Henry Edwards Huntington
His Life and His Collections

Henry Edwards Huntington
His Life and His Collections

A Docent Guide

Selena A. Spurgeon

Huntington Library
San Marino, California

A version of chapter five appeared in *Artnews* of March 1983 under the title "Old Masters and New Money."

© Copyright 1992 by Selena A. Spurgeon

Published by the Huntington Library
1151 Oxford Road, San Marino, California 91108

Printed in the United States of America

Spurgeon, Selena A., 1923-
    Henry Edwards Huntington: his life and his collections: a docent guide/ by Selena A. Spurgeon.
        p.   cm.
Includes index.
    1. Huntington, Henry Edwards, 1850-1927. 2. Henry E. Huntington Library and Art Gallery. 3. Rare books—Collectors and collecting—United States—History. 4. Art—Collectors and collecting—United States—History. 5. Capitalists and financiers—United States— Biography. 6. Book collectors—United States— Biography. I. Title.
Z989.H95S68 1992
002'.074'092—dc20
[B]   91-38241
                                                                          CIP

ISBN: 0-87328-137-3

An institution is the lengthened shadow
of one man.

from "Self-Reliance," *The Essays of Ralph Waldo Emerson*

Contents

Acknowledgments

This book contains information garnered during a long association with the Huntington. In September of 1972 I joined the first Library Docent Class and subsequently took those classes offered in the gardens and galleries. When a request came from the manuscript department for a volunteer, I eagerly applied and was able to work with the curators on the collections there. The Huntington family papers were brought together and catalogued and I was fortunate to be able to read them all and use the material in this book. Support has come from Henry Huntington's grandchildren and more distant relatives, from Dorothy Duveen Burns who graciously shared many anecdotes concerning her father, from readers, and from a multitude of staff members in all areas, many of whom have now died or retired.

This book is dedicated with love and gratitude to all my Huntington friends.

Selena A. Spurgeon

The Early Years   I

"I shall keep [Collis Huntington's] wise life as an example constantly before me."
                                    Henry Edwards Huntington, August 30, 1900

The Huntington family traced its ancestry back to the colonial days in America and in England to 1273. The member of whom they were most proud was Samuel Huntington (1731-96), governor and chief justice of Connecticut, president of the Continental Congress, and a signer of the Declaration of Independence. For generations the Huntingtons had been small landowners, merchants, self-reliant men and women who worked hard to make a living and thriftily to lay some aside. When Solon Huntington, father of Henry E. Huntington, died in 1890, the estimated value of his estate was $126,180, an important sum then in an isolated country town.

Throughout Henry Huntington's lifetime, he retained a deep love for his boyhood home, Oneonta, on the Susquehanna River in upper New York State. Here Solon had opened up a general store, taking his younger brother Collis into partnership. As the farming community grew, the business prospered, and soon Solon was able to invest some of his profits in land. He was also able to equip his ambitious brother Collis with merchandise to trade to the fortune hunters lured to the gold fields in California.

By the 1860s, Collis's California activities had expanded to that of building—along with his partners Charles Crocker,

Mark Hopkins, and Leland Stanford—the Central Pacific Railroad across the Sierra. At Promontory Point, Utah territory, this miracle of engineering and Congressional backing connected with the Union Pacific out over Indian lands from Omaha, the last link of the long-awaited transcontinental railroad. Vast tracts of agricultural and grazing land were thus opened for development.

On May 10, 1869, when the golden spike was driven connecting the tracks between east and west, Henry Huntington was a young man of nineteen. He had been born on February 27, 1850, the fourth of seven children. Within the family circle, he was always called Edward or Edwards, occasionally Ed. Mary Leonora was the eldest sister; an admired older brother, Howard, had died of a mysterious fever as a teenager; and George, next in line, lived only five years, leaving Henry Edwards the eldest surviving son. A younger brother, Willard, although better educated than the other sons through Uncle Collis's generosity, could never succeed in any of his endeavors; and there is no further information about little Harriet, other than that she was born in 1852 and died two years later. The youngest sister, Carrie, was closest to Henry Edwards, his confidante, constant correspondent, and ultimately the conscientious executrix of his will. Harriet Saunders Huntington, mother of the family, was particularly attached to her elder son and kept in close touch with him all her life through weekly letters, regular visits, and many worries over his well-being. Solon became a shadowy father, eclipsed by Collis's influence in all his relatives' affairs and particularly in those of his nephew Edwards. But Harriet insisted on her son's finishing high school and her interest in books, music, and the arts does much to explain his later acquisitions.

There is scant mention of Henry Edwards's boyhood days, as he was not prone to boast or reminisce. In later life when asked to authorize a biography, he would answer that his library would be his memorial. However, he once related an anecdote of early entrepreneurship to a journalist friend.

When he was a child of eight or nine, a circus came to town. There were various booths set up for refreshments and he managed to find a shed from which to sell candy, peanuts, and lemonade. A farmer provided competition, underselling him with drinks of cider from a large barrel. Young Edwards proceeded to buy the contents of the barrel for 10c a gallon, which he then sold to the crowds at 5c a glass. His profits came to $8.55 which, he said, looked bigger than anything he had made since.

Few luxuries were available in Oneonta, and no higher education, although the latter was not considered a drawback. In a 1910 letter, Huntington wrote, "the four or five years spent within college walls did not . . . yield at all a dividend commensurate with the loss sustained . . . in learning a busi-ness[,] as then the mind is plastic, the memory is retentive, and the habits of business permanently formed." He also did not believe that luck played any part in a man's life; good fortune depended on hard work and watchfulness for the great oppor-tunity. "Luck is simply another name for vigilance" was a favorite saying.

The spectacular success of the Central Pacific behind him, Collis Huntington, ever restless and ready for a new challenge, became involved in new ventures. Work with his partners started on a transcontinental route through Southern Califor-nia to New Orleans called the Southern Pacific Railroad; on his own he toyed briefly with the idea of constructing a subway system for New York City; shortly after he traveled to White Sulphur Springs, West Virginia, to take over the ailing Chesa-peake and Ohio Railroad with its terminus at Newport News, Virginia. Because of the expansion of this line, a position was opened for a hard-working, loyal associate.

Collis and his wife Elizabeth were childless although a niece, Clara, lived with them, whom they treated as a daugh-ter. Soon Collis became interested in his promising young nephew. At age twenty-one Henry Edwards was working dili-gently but unhappily as a porter in a New York City hardware store. His weekly letters home show him to be of a religious nature, eager to please, and very homesick. "I tell you, Mother, a boy knows how to appreciate Father and Mother when he gets away from home."

Wages in New York were uncertain, expensive dental work had been postponed, his clothes were wearing out, and his watch entrusted to his father for sale. Yet the young man was determined to succeed on his own without help from his prosperous uncle, then also living in the city. "I am getting to the age when I do not like to feel dependent on any one."

His self-reliance impressed Collis and so, in April 1871, Henry Edwards went to work for his uncle at $150 per month operating a sawmill near St. Albans, West Virginia, which supplied crossties and bridges for the Chesapeake and Ohio Railroad. The same trait is demonstrated in a letter he wrote back to Oneonta, about an experience he had when a rising river threatened the lumber for which he was responsible: "I had 50 rafts of timber in the river and did not lose but one log. . . . Some parties have lost three or four thousand dollars worth . . . but I showed them different. . . . I did save all my timber and the inhabitants say it is something that has never been done before." Thus Collis found a surrogate for the son and heir for which he had long envied his partners, a young man who would make his endeavors worthwhile. Their close relationship was to continue with only a short intermission for almost thirty years and was to influence the younger Huntington's personal and business practices for the rest of his life.

In November 1873, at Newark, New Jersey, Henry Edwards married Mary Alice Prentice, the older sister of Clara Prentice Huntington, the niece whom Collis and his wife had taken to live with them. The bond was almost certainly sponsored by the couple's uncle, who always had a dominant hand in the lives of his family. The newlyweds settled into a tiny cottage in West Virginia near the sawmill, and from here Mary wrote to her mother-in-law, "I cannot refrain from saying over again that we are indeed truly happy in our new home. . . . It makes me feel eager to be a good housekeeper as Edward seems pleased with my feeble efforts. I shall strive to improve!" Their only son, Howard, was born in St. Albans in 1876. In 1878, Clara Leonora arrived, followed by Elizabeth in 1880 (born in a house in Oneonta owned by Collis Huntington), and three years later Marian Prentice, born in 1883, completed the family group.

Henry Huntington and another young man named S. P. Franchot had bought a financial interest in the sawmill. It was an unhappy partnership since Franchot proved irresponsible. It was also embarrassing since his father, General Richard Franchot, was a family friend from upstate New York who was, at that time, a congressman from Schenectady, earning a salary of $20,000 a year as chief lobbyist for the Central Pacific. Huntington found the situation very upsetting. In a letter to his mother on August 23, 1874, he concluded his discussion of the matter with the underlined phrase, "End of it say no more about it for I don't like to think about it."

Franchot was finally bought out, partially paid with $1,800 worth of books from Huntington's personal library. It is interesting that Huntington was a book collector even from these early days. The books included a fifteen-volume leather-bound set of Dickens, twenty-five leather-bound volumes of Scott, an eight-volume leather-bound set of Bancroft's *History*, *The Life and Works of William Cowper* by Robert Southey in eight cloth-bound volumes, and biographies of Aaron Burr and Andrew Jackson.

Huntington continued to operate the mill for a year on his own and it was then sold for a profit. After a few years back in Oneonta helping his aging father with some business ventures, he returned to work for his uncle. Their relationship, as seen through their correspondence, is full of mutual esteem and understanding. During the time he worked as a superintendent of construction for the Chesapeake, Ohio, and Southwestern Railway between Tennessee and Kentucky in 1882, he wrote to his mother about some of his feelings toward Collis:

"I have never worked harder than I have on this work nor have more to contend with and I cannot tell you how gratified I am that he appreciated it and I feel fully repaid for my labor." Collis on his part wrote, "No better boy than Ed ever lived."

Henry Edwards, with his cheerful nature, his ability to build a loyal and efficient work force through his own dawn-to-dusk working habits, and his insistence upon high standards in the maintenance of roads and equipment, often served as a mediator for his blustery outspoken uncle. He was not driven by social or political ambitions, but became first a trusted colleague and then obvious heir apparent, subordinating his own ambitions to those of aiding his uncle, but learning and evaluating at the same time until finally he could put his drive to work for his own purposes. He matured rapidly, began to accumulate a little capital of his own, and was soon known to financiers and railroad people on both coasts. To differentiate between the two Huntingtons, they called them "C. P." and "H. E."

In 1890 Collis Huntington was elected president of the Southern Pacific Company to replace ousted Leland Stanford. Stanford was then running for senator from California and was putting most of his energy toward opening, on the family farm at Palo Alto, the university that bears his son's name; he had long been little more than a figurehead in charge of public relations for the company. Two years later, to keep an eye on the Southern Pacific headquarters while he was occupied in the east and to handle the company's street railway business, Collis put Henry Huntington in charge of the Southern Pacific Company with headquarters in San Francisco. This proved to be a difficult post for he had to contend with the jealousies of the large railroad stockholders, but it did mark Henry Huntington's first experience of California.

En route to his new office at Post and Montgomery streets in San Francisco, he stopped briefly in Los Angeles. The layover came in the spring of 1892, when the hills were green and the wild flowers in bloom. He was invited by rancher J. deBarth Shorb to visit his estate "San Marino" outside the city. Huntington was entranced by his surroundings and the friendliness of the people.

From Collis's personal bank account, H. E. Huntington was paid $10,000 a year for his new position, and his salary was soon raised to $12,500. In San Francisco, he and his wife Mary were able to buy a fine house containing three stories, with a billiard room in the basement and several servants' rooms, at 2849 Jackson Street (the numbers were changed following the holocaust of 1906). Judging from a list of furniture from the house, the couple lived in comfort and in style, far removed from the circumstances of the West Virginia cottage where a packing crate with boards nailed across for shelves had served as a china cabinet. A flat library table, purchased at the same time as the furniture for the house, was sent to the office—the first of a notable collection.

In the 1890s, the Henry Huntingtons became prominent in the social life of San Francisco, joining the Burlingame Country Club and entertaining friends and relatives from the east. Mary joined a group of ladies raising funds for the Children's Hospital. She took her daughters, by now in their teens, to Europe, the first of many trips of sightseeing and visiting her sister, who was now the Princess Clara Huntington Hatzfeldt, the wife of a German nobleman. Young Howard had started working for various railroads at age fourteen: it was not until he was twenty-four and had been instructed by private tutors that he went across the country to Harvard to study engineering. Here, true to the family tradition, he left college, arguing that he had "passed beyond the schoolboy stage" and would learn more by devoting his time to his father's business. The eldest daughter, Clara, became the artist who is represented by a marble relief of Huntington in the Pavilion entry of the Library and by a statue of St. Francis beside the lily ponds in the gardens.

In 1896 and '97, Henry Huntington, now approaching fifty, was nearly overcome with illness and fatigue from the pressures of work. His daughter Clara wrote that he "looked dreadfully," his secretary sent a conspiratorial letter to Collis suggesting a visit east be extended as long as possible for a good rest, his wife Mary was alarmed enough to hope for a few weeks' vacation in the mountains, and the newspapers hinted at a nervous breakdown. But there was no respite; he was indispensable at company headquarters in San Francisco. He instituted several policies to raise the railroad's profits, among them reducing the huge number of free passes previously allocated and practicing economies in all areas. Naturally, this frugality created many enemies and, while Collis was three thousand miles away in New York, he found that the title of aide-to-the-president carried little status.

Collis wrote encouragingly in November 1897, "if you keep right on the way you have been doing, I think it will be right with everybody; if it is not, it will be right in itself, and that will be a great satisfaction to you, as it will to me." But Henry Huntington replied to his uncle: "My inclination for some time has been to resign. . . . I am not sure but that it would be better for you if I did. . . . I am getting very tired."

One of the few bright spots during these harried years was a newspaper column, carefully preserved among the Huntington correspondence, from the *Evening Express* of San Francisco, November 6, 1897, in which the columnist wrote, "Whatever may be said about the Huntington influence, it cannot be denied that it has transformed the Southern Pacific from a very wild, wooly, and western road into, as far as discipline and business goes, one the equal of the best managed Eastern lines, and this has largely been done by Henry E. Huntington, the nephew. . . . He has one quality which all of his associates in the management of the road do not possess, and that is politeness." This trait and those of tact, graciousness, and "sweetness of thought" were remarked upon throughout his life.

Collis died suddenly of heart failure at age seventy-nine on August 13, 1900, at his lodge at Raquette Lake in the Adirondack Mountains. Henry Huntington was then supervising the grading and construction of the Houston and Texas Central

Railroad, one of the branch lines that consolidated the Southern Pacific's interests in that state. He was rushed by private car with absolute right-of-way to the funeral at the Collis Huntington town-house at Fifty-seventh Street and Fifth Avenue in New York. He was devastated, and the shock was one he bore alone: his wife Mary was in Europe at the time on one of her frequent visits and did not return until several months later. In answer to letters of condolence, he wrote that he had lost "friend, uncle, father—everything that stands for affection and unvarying goodness of heart."

In his lengthy will, with bequests to all family members, Collis paid special tribute to his nephew. To his second wife, Arabella, along with many other considerations, went two-thirds of his Southern Pacific capital stock, a total of 259,800 shares, appraised at $8,703,318.98. To Henry Edwards Huntington went the other one-third of his Southern Pacific stock, 129,000 shares appraised at $4,351,659.49. He and Arabella divided the residue of the estate, she receiving the majority and, thus, they each acquired an interest in the Newport News Shipbuilding and Drydock Company, into which Collis had poured money and energy during his final years. Henry Huntington's share, in bonds and preferred stock of Newport News, totaled $4,868,623.34, and he also received $1,311,663.02 in cash and almost $2,500,000 in additional properties. There were three executors of the will, including Arabella. Although heartbroken, she was now anxious to learn as much as possible of the complex holdings from the other appointees and from her nephew-by-marriage, Henry Edwards. It took several years of his time and many trips to New York before the estate was finally settled.

It was generally taken for granted that Henry Huntington, with his vast experience as first vice president and as heir to a large percentage of the stock, would assume the presidency of the Southern Pacific Company. But he was opposed by many of the major stockholders, including an English bloc which resented his economies and felt that, following Collis's custom of plowing money back into the company, Henry Huntington, too, would be reluctant to pay out future dividends. An outsider from Canada was chosen for the position, with Edward Henry Harriman taking control of the executive committee of the Southern Pacific Company.

Harriman, a year older than Henry Huntington, was the son of a poor minister and, with scant schooling, had gone to work in a stock exchange office at age fourteen. Aided by a photographic memory, fine powers of persuasion, and a superb intellect, he became one of the most powerful figures on Wall Street. In 1897 he had helped with the refinancing of the Union Pacific Railroad and the next year became chairman of this road which, under his administration, quickly showed a profit and expanded its facilities.

Harriman had had previous dealings with Collis Huntington but no stock had changed hands. Collis had looked upon the Central Pacific as his private property, to be treasured at any cost. He had written a warning letter to his nephew on October 20, 1899, "I had a long talk with Harriman about overland matters. . . . We had a long and very pleasant talk, but he, you know, is very sharp and sometimes I think I am hardly capable of trading with him in regards to these matters."

In January 1901, Henry Huntington and Arabella sold their shares of Southern Pacific stock to Harriman who, in 1902, assumed presidency of that company. With his control of the Union Pacific, Harriman now had a direct outlet to the west coast via the Central Pacific, under the ownership of the Southern Pacific.

It was not often that the Southern Pacific stock could be disposed of on such favorable terms. In the months since Collis's death, with the promise of higher dividends in the offing, the stock had soared and Henry Huntington's shares increased in value from the August appraisal to $6,689,864.42, a gain of about a third and a huge profit in which Arabella also participated. Collis had a clause in his will stating that "such shares should not, in whole or in part, be disposed of, during the lifetime of either, except with the consent of both legatees or the survivors of them."

When the stock sale was made public, an old California friend, Frank Miller of Riverside, lamented, "All California color and spirit has left the organization. . . . Seriously, what made you do it?" There were many facets to the answer. Although Henry Huntington remained as vice president until 1910 and was proud to be a director of the Southern Pacific for the rest of his life, the zest had gone, and he turned his thoughts from San Francisco to Southern California. He remembered his pleasant associations there and his good health in what he termed a more "polite climate." But primarily he saw the vast potential for development in the southern part of the state, using his own initiative and capital. His domestic arrangements in the north were deteriorating and so he instituted proceedings to sell his large holdings in the Market Street Railway of San Francisco and contacted a Los Angeles realtor to look for a suitable dwelling.

Building the Fortune   II

*"I traveled east, north and south from one end of the state to another.
I came to the conclusion then that the greatest natural advantages,
those of climate and every other condition, lay in Southern California
and that is why I made it the field of my endeavor."*
                        Henry Huntington, quoted in the *Los Angeles Examiner,*
                                                    November 27, 1908

At the time Henry Huntington moved to Southern California,
the 1900 census had given the city of Los Angeles 102,479 residents. Over ninety years later the estimate approaches
3,500,000. Much of the early growth of the city and the areas
around it can be attributed to the creation of an interurban
railway system, the Pacific Electric Company, which became
the largest in the world. Fifty communities from Santa Monica
to Balboa were connected along the Pacific Ocean and stretching inland to Redlands, Pasadena, and the San Fernando Valley. Nearly one hundred individual transportation firms were
consolidated into one corporation, achieving Huntington's
boast, "We will join this whole region into one big family."
    While working in San Francisco, Huntington had been
involved with the street railways, converting them from horsedrawn vehicles to electric trolleys. In 1898, feeling that this
experience could be profitably expanded southward, he, together with Collis Huntington and some other business leaders, purchased a bankrupt interurban line called the Los Angeles and Pasadena Railway Company—often referred to as the

Short Line. In November of 1901 this company was divided between a city streetcar line and interurban components, with Henry Huntington president and largest stockholder of each. The Pacific Light and Power Company was formed under the auspices of the Los Angeles Railway to provide electricity for the trolleys as well as for residential use.

The interurban railway system was built with standard gauge tracks of 4′ 8$^{1}/_{2}$″ rather than the considerably narrower tracks used by the city streetcars. Thus the outlying passenger and freight cars could be interchanged with those of the steam railways and compete with their business. It became evident, when the trolley franchise was bought in Ventura, that the objective of the Pacific Electric was to extend service up the coast to Santa Barbara and beyond to the inland agricultural valleys. The tracks, in many cases, paralleled those acquired by Harriman's Southern Pacific. One of his secretaries wrote, "There is a good deal of talk about Mr. Huntington running his trolley lines to 'Frisco'. It looks a little like hot air but I would hardly be surprised if such a thing did happen within the next year, would you?" Another ambitious but unrealized goal was the extension of Pacific Electric lines down the coast to San Diego. This expansion was blocked by Harriman because the plans conflicted with the long-range objectives railways of his Southern Pacific.

To help cope with the climate of intrigue and financial finagling that existed in the railroad circles of the 1890s, a code was used by C. P. Huntington and H. E. Huntington when communicating by telegraph between their offices in New York and San Francisco and later from Los Angeles, as freight and passenger rivalry became intense between the Pacific Electric and the Southern Pacific. Ciphered messages were also used when Huntington was juggling accounts and buying and paying for books and art objects for the San Marino collections and commenting on other sensitive subjects. His code name was "Saxon."

Knowing which way the transit lines were to be laid,

Huntington was able to purchase large tracts of acreage in the paths of greatest progress. It was almost exclusively through the sale of real estate that Huntington was able to augment many times over his inherited fortune. His organizational skills of buying, consolidating, and disposing of unnecessary appendages were clearly part of the business practices he had learned from the many years of close association with his beloved Uncle Collis. By July 1902 the Big Red Cars of the Pacific Electric sped along tracks to Long Beach, a connection that revitalized that city, whose inhabitants quickly adapted to the convenience of over one hundred round trips daily to Los Angeles. This scenario was repeated over and over again as small towns and uninhabited areas were joined together and opened to growth and prosperity. Many large landowners donated rights-of-way through their properties as they envisioned the benefits to follow when their acreage was subdivided.

Another line, the Los Angeles Interurban Railway, independently organized in June 1904 by Henry Huntington and later leased to the Pacific Electric Company, ran down the coast from Huntington Beach to Newport and the Balboa Peninsula. It did not enter Los Angeles but connected with tracks that did project into the city. Various of the Huntington-controlled land companies bought up properties in the beach cities where land values later exploded. The Redondo Land Company was bought: this brought with it ownership of ninety percent of the land in Redondo as well as the Los Angeles and Redondo Railway. Another boom resulted and Huntington became the largest landowner, and the largest taxpayer, in Southern California.

On July 13, 1905, Edmund Burke Holladay, who had married Huntington's sister Carrie, described the scene: "On Friday last it came out in the paper that Mr. H. E. Huntington had bought the entire town site of Redondo from the Redondo Land Company and that he would offer it for sale. And—Oh! what a change in the twinkling of an eye—immediately the people of Los Angeles rushed down in droves to Redondo to

buy, buy, buy. . . . The name of Huntington had done it all—
Prices of land, bought two weeks ago at $1500—sold for say
$4000 and again for $6000. One piece of land, which Edwards
told the real estate man was worth $15,000—and at which he
laughed—was later bought for $22,000—and so on. . . . Ed-
wards couldn't keep away and much of the time stood or sat
by his agents, smiling and helping the good work along. . . .
On Monday afternoon we went out to Redondo once again—
no longer the 'Dead Town,' but now 'Redondo the Beautiful.'. . .
I never saw or heard so sincere or unanimous a compliment to
one man's judgement as this sudden and absolute change of
opinion about Redondo—a place which for years was con-
demned as not desirable in one hour is changed to be the most
desirable spot known—and not scores—but hundreds and
thousands of people with money are madly struggling to get
each a small piece."

The Redondo boom lost its momentum rapidly but, in a
few frantic weeks, Huntington had sold approximately
$3,000,000 worth of real estate there, recouping what he had
paid for the land and for the previously independent Los
Angeles and Redondo Railway. He then purchased 3,000 additional acres of farm property in the neighborhood. He built
loading wharves along the shoreline, a pavilion auditorium,
and a huge indoor saltwater swimming pool, large enough for
two thousand bathers at one time. A surfer performed twice
daily in the ocean to the amazement of the crowds. The Plunge
was warmed from the outflow of Huntington's Station Z, the
Pacific Light and Power Plant located a mile away.

Weekends and holidays were a popular time to ride the
Big Red Cars. Whole families, rich and poor, enjoyed the great
circle trips for a very small fare, usually a dollar a head, to see
the sights of Southern California. Huntington considered pleasure and a good life in his adopted state as important as financial advantage. One popular outing was to the historical
Mission San Gabriel, founded in 1771 by the Franciscan Fathers
who came from Mexico under the direction of Fr. Junipero

Serra. The trip also included a look at the Ostrich Farm in South Pasadena which flourished at a time when ladies wore elaborate hats. Adults and children delighted in feeding the ostriches large oranges and watching the outlines of the fruit slowly descend the necks of the exotic birds. The most exciting journey of all was on the Mount Lowe Excursion Line acquired by the Pacific Electric in 1901. Passengers would come out on the red cars to Altadena, above Pasadena, to join a cable railroad which rose through a system of weights to Echo Mountain. Here they transferred to narrow gauge trolleys and rode around sharp curves and over wooden trestles to Mount Lowe, almost a mile high. Disembarking, they could dine in the hotel, eventually destroyed by fire in the 1930s, or spend the night in a cabin before returning. The spectacular view of fifty-six cities could be admired and the contrast in climate proved exhilarating for, in winter, the route was often covered with snow.

As president of the Pacific Electric and of the Los Angeles Railway, Henry Huntington took a pride in his work that was very personal, not measured by time or dollars. Affectionately known by his employees as the "Old Man," he was an early riser and out at daybreak looking over his lines. His passion for maps, specifications, and newspaper clippings led him to carry his records with him for easy perusal and he was seldom without bulging pockets stuffed with information to assist what was already a phenomenal memory. Following Collis's custom, he rarely took a vacation and found his only recreation in fierce games of dominoes with his lawyer William Dunn and his doctor Ernest Bryant, while son Howard had a large handicap in the competition.

Wages in 1901 were eighteen cents an hour for starting motormen and conductors, while the more experienced employees took home twenty-two cents. In May 1903, all workers with the Los Angeles Railway were rewarded for their loyalty in repudiating union organizational tactics with a special promotion of two years in seniority on the service list. Henry

Huntington heartily distrusted all labor unions after strikers had disrupted traffic and burned bridges when he was working in San Francisco. When the "Old Man" raised beginning pay to twenty-two cents an hour for a ten-hour-day and a six-day week—totaling an annual $686.40 with no extra for overtime, holidays, or sick pay—the news was extraordinary enough to warrant an impromptu celebration at the trolley barns, attended by Huntington and Howard, who was then assistant general manager of the Los Angeles Railway.

In 1896, Maria de Jesus Shorb and her husband James deBarth Shorb, Huntington's host on his first visit to Southern California, found it necessary to mortgage their ranch of some 550 acres when disease laid waste to their vineyards. Shorb died soon after and, in 1899, the California Superior Court foreclosed on the mortgage. On January 2, 1903, the estate was sold to the Huntington Land and Improvement Company for $239,729.94. At first it had been called the Los Robles Ranch but the name was changed to San Marino in recognition of Shorb's ancestral home in Maryland: it became the site of Henry Huntington's future residence and much of the city of San Marino.

Henry Huntington's neighbor to the west, on the Lake Vineyard Ranch, was George S. Patton. Patton became a trusted friend and eventually managed the Huntington Land and Improvement Company and became land agent for the Pacific Electric. He was related to many of the old Los Angeles families. His father-in-law was Benjamin D. Wilson, a great landowner and first official mayor of Los Angeles. Patton was the father of the World War II general George S. Patton, Jr., who grew up on the Lake Vineyard property and, in 1945, presented a copy of Hitler's *Mein Kampf* to the Huntington Library.

Above the Patton estate, on the outskirts of Pasadena, was a thirty-acre wooded plateau where construction had begun on a luxurious resort hotel. Unforeseen building costs and heavy rains landed the hotel in receivership before it was completed and eventually it had to be sold for taxes. Huntington found it "offensive to the eye" but saw the business opportunities in promoting a first-rate hotel and tourist attraction situated on the Pacific Electric Line. He bought the land and unfinished structure and, with the assistance of an experienced Pasadena hotel man, Daniel Moore Linnard, the building was finished. Two stories were added by the architect Myron Hunt, and the hotel was landscaped by William Hertrich, both involved in Huntington's own house and gardens at the San Marino Ranch. Opening to the public in January 1914 in time for the four-month winter season, the hotel quickly became popular with visitors from the east. It was renamed the Huntington Hotel and remained under Huntington's ownership until May 3, 1917.

In 1903 Henry Huntington exchanged 40,326.66 shares of Pacific Electric stock with Harriman's Southern Pacific for some valuable rights-of-way. Harriman's ownership thus then equaled that of Huntington, with three San Francisco financiers holding the balance. Huntington was delighted with the arrangement, which he felt insured the future of the company, and wrote his mother, "I have won all my battles now."

This contract between Huntington and Harriman had an important paragraph with far-reaching implications. It gave the privilege of first purchase to the remaining parties if any stockholder wanted to sell. When tracks were laid down in the Covina area to the east of Los Angeles and to Whittier to the southeast, the rights-of-way were unexpectedly costly, since they passed through, and destroyed, commercial walnut groves. Other large assessments came due during these depression years and the Northern California partners became discouraged with the seemingly hopeless venture. The large financial demands were deemed unmanageable and they declined participation in any further proceedings. They offered their 19,346.68 shares in the Pacific Electric Company to Huntington and Harriman, who divided them equally.

On December 14, 1904, Huntington wrote Harrison Gray Otis, founder of the *Los Angeles Times,* "I have purchased the interest of those from whom opposition has been encountered in the past and might be expected in the future and I think that this is a good guarantee that we shall keep doing business at the old stand and going forward all the time. I am more than ever impressed with the fact that when you have on hand a big proposition that is found to require strong and continuous waiting you don't want to handicap yourself with companions who get cold feet, however excellent may be the gentlemen themselves."

It would be to Huntington's eternal disappointment that he had misjudged the willingness of his San Francisco colleagues to accomplish their common goals. He had lost his buffer with Harriman and disagreements were constant. Years before, Collis Huntington had emphasized that what he could not control, he would not own; he would take orders from no man. Thus dual ownership in the Pacific Electric was distasteful to Henry Huntington, who had thrived on independence and knew full well the tensions of complicated partnerships.

In June 1908, he began systematically selling and trading his interests in various lines and lands, properties that might at one time have been key parts of his projected statewide railway plan. In November of 1910, the transaction was complete and what is known as "The Great Merger" was accomplished. William Herrin, chief counsel of the Southern Pacific, became president of the Pacific Electric under the auspices of the Southern Pacific Railroad after Harriman died in 1909.

Huntington took full control of the Los Angeles Railway, and continued in this capacity until his death, although in later years much of the administrative work was done by Howard and attorney William Dunn. The trolleys were not as much affected as the red interurban cars of the Pacific Electric system by the increase in automotive travel, and the number of the narrow-gauge routes expanded. He considered some offers to sell after Howard's death in 1922 and wrote to Dunn, "the property has a very bright future. I expect as far as I am personally concerned, it would be better for me to keep the property, but as you know I want to get out of active business and fool away money on books and other things that give me pleasure."

After his death in 1927, the Los Angeles Railway was held by his estate until 1944, when it was sold to a subsidiary of the National City Lines. This later became the Los Angeles Transit Line and the old trolleys were gradually replaced with buses. The Big Red Cars of the interurban system operated until 1963, when special trips were featured for trolley buffs, but finally taps was sounded. Today there is hope that the rail system will be reactivated to solve the region's mounting transit problems.

The heaviest business pressures had already been disposed of by the time of "The Great Merger," when Huntington observed his sixtieth birthday. His semi-retirement brought out a wealth of underlying interests which he had never before had the time to indulge. He began to devote his energies to building up the San Marino Ranch. Finishing one challenge, he moved on to apply his business tactics to other purposes, to create the remarkable Huntington Library, Art Collections, and Botanical Gardens.

The Home   III

"I am more than ever persuaded that this is the only place in the world to live."

Henry E. Huntington, San Marino, January 23, 1922

In 1905, as befitting the president of the Pacific Electric Company, a special railway car was built for Huntington's private use. It was painted dark green on the outside and lettered only with "Private" and "The Alabama." The interior walls were paneled in mahogany, there were silk shades on the lighting fixtures, and a dining room that seated ten around an inlaid table. There was even a wood-burning fireplace. The top speed of one hundred miles per hour was seldom tested, as the car was used sedately by Huntington to survey the far reaches of his interurban empire. When asked by his children the significance of the name "The Alabama," he answered that it came from the Indian language and meant the same as Oneonta. In reality, Alabama was the state that his Uncle Collis's widow claimed as her birthplace and it was a railroad man's finest compliment to name his magnificent car in her honor.

The year 1906 marked several important changes in Henry Huntington's life. It was the year of the devastating San Francisco earthquake and fire. The house on Nob Hill that Collis had bought for Arabella and extensively remodeled was completely destroyed. The only known personal letter of any content between Huntington and Arabella dates from this period, written to "My dear Bell" and signed "With much love to you, I remain your aff neph Edwards." It concerns the fire damage to the house, the contents of which were fully insured. Of great worry to both was the William Keith photograph of Collis, taken a few months before his death; it was eventually found at a neighbor's house. Four paintings were recovered, but the rest of the valuable art collection was lost. Henry Huntington purchased two of the four, of the Barbizon School, after Arabella's death and hung them upstairs at the Ranch. Today, *Milking Time* by Constant Tryon and *Homeward Bound* by Emil Van Marke decorate Friends' Hall in the entrance pavilion. Two Canary Island date palms survived the fire, with the trunks and fronds severely burned. Henry Huntington had them boxed, each weighing eighteen tons, loaded onto a flatbed Southern Pacific freight car, and brought to the San Marino Ranch, where one still stands in the palm garden, visible from the house.

Huntington was at this time frequently traveling east to help Arabella with her business affairs, but in 1906 another trip was also necessary when his mother, Harriet Saunders Huntington, died at the age of eighty-four. She had been in poor health and lately spending her winters with her daughter, Caroline Holladay, in San Francisco. When the weather warmed up and the orchard came into bloom, it was her custom to return home to Oneonta. For years her devoted son had urged her, "We want you to have everything in the world you want. The only trouble is you don't want much." After years of frugal living, her only indulgence was a piano, which she had purchased only shortly before her death.

Harriet was buried next to Solon Huntington and those of their children who had died young. One of the clauses in Henry Huntington's will contained instructions to provide $5,000 for perpetual care of the cemetery plot. The surviving brothers and sisters divided the contents of the house, Henry giving most of his share to Carrie, but taking from his mother's bedroom a photograph of himself and Collis standing together. From the parlor he chose two old framed eighteenth-century pictures, prints of *The Red Boy* and *The Blue Boy*, and another of an unidentified Gainsborough, perhaps *The Duchess of Cumberland*, now with *The Blue Boy* in the Huntington Collection. (*The Red Boy* was likely Lawrence's *Master Lambton*, which was widely reproduced at the time.) The house was given to the city of Oneonta where, with some additional land, it is used today as a park and the town library, with a fine memorial stone at the entrance.

Also in the spring of 1906, Henry Huntington and his wife, Mary Alice, were divorced. They had been separated at least as early as 1900 when he was constantly engrossed in business on both coasts and she was spending much of her time with her sister in England and at the Continental spas. Most of the correspondence concerning the divorce was destroyed but two revealing letters from Henry Huntington remain, addressed to Elizabeth, the second daughter. The first is dated February 11, 1906, and concerns her just announced engagement to John Brockway Metcalf: "My darling daughter —Yours received and you have finally decided on a date I cannot tell you how happy I hope you will be and believe you will be for I feel that you and Brockway are congenial If a person is happily married, life is just beginning You must both be patient with each other and give up to each other When one always gives up to the other it is very apt to make the one given up to very selfish My dear child I don't think it is necessary for me to advise you for you are so self sacrificing but you will be happier if you do not carry it to [*sic*] far. I speak knowingly and feelingly With all the love in the world for my dear child I am as ever Your affectionate Father." (The punctuation is Huntington's.)

A few weeks later, on March 22, 1906, he wrote again to his daughter, now honeymooning in Japan: "My darling daughter—Before this reaches you, you will undoubtedly have learned of the separation of your mother and myself I can never tell you how much I regret that this cloud should come into your life but I hope it may have a silver lining. As you of course know we have been very unhappy for years and getting more so as the years went by The step taken seemed inevitable and the sooner it was taken the better it would be for all concerned I think we shall all be much happier after the clouds pass over and that peace will come to us. Nothing could have been worse than it has been and I felt like a wanderer on the face of the earth, without a home or a place to lay my head I think now I shall build a home where my children can come when they desire and that many happy days will come to me and all mine. I have never talked with you about your mother and my relations. You could not but see however how unhappy I have been but no one ever knew how much I have suffered I would have liked to have talked the matter over with you but thought it best to keep the matter from you as long as possible and not to mar the first pleasure of your wedding trip and thought it only fair to give your mother the opportunity to speak to you first You can never know my precious child how very dear my children are to me and how much I regret that I have not been able to make your lives happier I can only say I have done my best With a heart full of love for my dear child I am always Your affectionate Father."

There are no specific reasons for the incompatibility but evidence that Mary suffered from "intense nervousness," was reluctant to move from San Francisco to Los Angeles, and was upset and overly sympathetic when her little sister, the Princess Clara Hatzfeldt, did not receive a true daughter's share of Collis's estate—only a million dollars. (According to the *New York Times* of September 17, 1924, Arabella and Henry combined to settle the Princess's claims by jointly giving her $6,000,000.) Other rumors suggest trouble may have arisen from Arabella's intrusion in the marriage and the vast periods that Henry Huntington spent with her in arranging Collis's estate. The newspapers reported Mary's charge as desertion, and the hearing lasted a mere seven and a half minutes. The settlement included the Jackson Street house in San Francisco, $300,000 already in her name, monthly stipends for the four children, and a million dollars in trust at four percent annual interest that would revert to Henry Huntington after her death. Appearing nervous and attired in a steel-gray traveling costume, with her hat and face covered with a double veil, she left immediately after the decree with her youngest daughter, Marian, for a voyage to Japan to join the newly married Metcalfs, just missing the great San Francisco earthquake and fire the following month.

Henry Huntington had known his uncle's widow, Arabella, for the thirty years that they had loved and remained loyal to the same man. Since Collis's death, they were thrown together for months at a time, working out the details of his estate. Huntington's four children, now independent, were well aware of his devotion to their aunt and amused that their father was looking and acting like "a young sprig." In New York he changed his clothes three times a day, from a morning coat to a black cutaway and then to evening dress. Arabella was a stylish woman who demanded a well-groomed escort. Her sophistication and example turned a hard-working California railroad builder into a distinguished man of the world. Huntington admired her intelligence, her energy, and her vibrant personality as he had his uncle's. He was beguiled by her quest for beauty and found her excitingly different from the other women he had known.

In 1903 Arabella wrote to Carrie, "What is the matter with Edward? I heard he was well and strong and having a very gay time in Los Angeles, Give him my love and tell him to get well. All his troubles are imaginary. With his power to live, work, and do good, nothing should trouble him. I will write to him on some business matters tonight." Later, after his divorce, she again wrote Carrie, "I am sure everything will come out all right in the end. I worry for Edward simply because others have been so disagreeable. Fortunately, he is a man and can stand hard treatment." Soon it became obvious that they would marry although, in 1909, Arabella told inquisitive reporters, "You can say for me that I have no intention of marrying anyone. I shall sail for Europe on June 1st, there to remain a year. I hope no one will be so unkind to say that I am eloping with my little nephew."

The reasons for the length of the courtship are not apparent. Arabella's reluctance may have been caused by the thought of moving to a ranch amid the isolation of acres of orange groves in the wilderness of Southern California, far away from her son Archer. The newspapers had rumored a wedding for so many years that when it finally came about in 1913, it was a complete surprise to all but Huntington's sister Carrie, who had been let in on the secret. When Huntington went abroad for the first time and stayed at Claridge's in London, friends and family considered the trip strictly a book-buying event. He then went on to Paris, where Arabella was finally persuaded. Whatever the reasons for the delay, the marriage was a happy one but, like many marriages, one of compromises and a deeper commitment on one part than the other.

If the dates on the Huntington mausoleum are correct, both Henry and Arabella Huntington were sixty-three years of age when they married in 1913. There is no description of her at this time and no known posed photograph of the two together. However, his U.S. passport, issued April 16, 1913, describes him as follows:

Age-63
Stature-5ft.10^1/$_2$"
Forehead-High
Eyes-Blue
Nose-Straight
Mouth-Large
Chin-Prominent
Hair-White (bald)
Complexion-Fair
Face-Oval

He remained a handsome man, gradually putting on additional weight which he carried well due to his height and meticulously tailored clothing. His voice was low and he preferred to listen than to dominate a conversation. He was an unerring judge of men and, like his uncle, had infinite patience in consummating his business and personal desires.

In 1905, Henry Huntington had first met the architect Myron Hunt, when he went to Hunt's office to discuss plans for the houses he intended building for his eldest children on neighboring ten-acre plots in Pasadena. Huntington was, at this time, living alone in a suite of five rooms at the Jonathan Club in Los Angeles.

Myron Hunt had been born in 1868 in Massachusetts and had studied at Northwestern University and Massachusetts Institute of Technology. He had spent much time traveling and studying in Europe and returned to live in Chicago, where he became an admirer of Frank Lloyd Wright. He moved to Pasadena because of his wife's frail health and began an architectural career that took in a variety of Southern California buildings—the Rose Bowl, the Ambassador Hotel in Los Angeles, parts of the Mission Inn in Riverside, the La Jolla Art Gallery, the Pasadena Public Library, colleges, and countless commercial buildings, hospitals, and residences. Many of these he would supervise while they were under construction, riding on horseback from his Pasadena home to the various sites. From the start of his California career, he was foremost among the local architects and commanded higher fees than they did.

With the children's houses under construction, Henry Huntington mentioned to Hunt that he intended one day building on the Shorb place, on the site of the previous owner's home. The old house, first built in 1877 and subsequently enlarged with a third story, was magnificently situated about twelve miles inland from Los Angeles atop a knoll. The 360-degree view, with Mount Wilson and Mount Lowe to the north, snowcapped Mount Baldy to the northeast, the lovely Whittier Hills to the southeast, and the rolling fields of grain and citrus orchards stretching west to the city and beyond to the Pacific, was unsurpassed in all of Southern California.

Some pencil plans had been made in 1904 and 1905 by an engineer employed by the Pacific Electric Company. Nothing came of these early attempts but, in February 1908, Huntington wrote a formal letter to Hunt & Grey outlining his dream house—the museum that the public now knows as the Huntington Art Gallery. "I enclose herewith a rough sketch of the house which I think should be built at Los Robles (Shorb place), although I have not fully decided to do so. I would not want any material changes made in the plans but would be glad to have you make any suggestions that may occur to you. You will no doubt have to make some minor changes in the fireplaces, which I have indicated thus ▭ and in the windows. I think of building a fireproof house of reinforced concrete stucco finish. The style of architecture proposed when your Mr. Hunt was here, I think will be satisfactory. There should be an entrance way and a long hall and a stairway to the court in the rear, and be sure to have plenty of light in the hall. I want all the rooms white with the exception of the Library which I shall probably have finished in mahogany. There should be stationary bookcases, the tops of the doors of which should be eight feet from the floor. How would the dining room look with the sidewalls panelled to the ceiling? Did you not mention when here that this could be done in plaster. Perhaps, however, it would be cheaper in wood; possibly this might make a good finish for the hall also? All the bathrooms should be tiled, except the housekeeper's and the servants', the floor of which should be of hard wood. If single windows would look as well architecturally, I would prefer them as they could be more artistically draped. I would want hot water heating, and cellars under the whole house, and think I should want an equipment for vacuum cleaning. I am suggesting these details without regard for order. I expect to leave here for California about the middle of March and wish you would send me the ground plans and also a rough sketch of the elevation, as soon as you can possibly do so. Wire me on receipt of this when you will send them. Also send me a rough estimate as to what you think the house would cost. I am in great haste to get this so that I can study the plans before I leave." In New York, Arabella Huntington was consulted on every phase of the construction and he was eager to spread his ideas before her.

The plan was U-shaped, with two wings connected by a long hall running through the center rooms. Hunt thought this reminiscent of a hotel and suggested that the hall be placed on the north side to let in more light and to accentuate the sweeping double staircase. To finalize the plans, Hunt traveled to New York and, during one long afternoon and evening session at the Metropolitan Club, the rough draft was agreed upon. On another New York trip, when the plans and specifications were written up and the contract ready to be signed, Huntington came in hurriedly in evening clothes and quickly placed his name on the last page. Hunt was aghast at the haste and seeming unconcern and asked, "Why, Mr. Huntington, aren't you going to read it to see if it is all right?" Huntington answered in a joking way as he went out the door, "If it isn't, I'll fire you." When doing business with a man whose reputation and integrity had been thoroughly researched, he would trust him completely.

The stucco-finished Huntington home is neoclassical or Beaux Arts in design, but Hunt had no easily recognizable trademark; each of his buildings was distinctive in its own right. He was interested also in the site, and the use of proper landscaping to unite the house and garden. His skill in earth-moving to enhance a setting must have sparked a special admiration, for, in October 1904, Huntington had written his mother, "I am doing some grading on the Shorb place. You know I can't well live unless I am grading someplace." But with a few exceptions Hunt did not participate in the landscaping around the Huntington house; the patio he had envisioned between the U-shaped wings of the house was never developed and the main entrance there seldom used. It was Huntington's trusted superintendent, William Hertrich, who was responsible for most of the lawns and gardens.

In the fall of 1908, excavation began for the huge basement, large enough to accommodate eight horses hitched to a road plow. The alignment of the house had to be altered in order to save two large live oaks, thus shifting slightly the north-south, east-west axes of the foundation upon which the already planted rose garden and north vista had been predicated. There was no modern machinery and the wagons for dirt moving had to be loaded by hand. Huntington was often on the grounds and derived great pleasure from watching the construction. The story goes that one day a load of material was brought in without sufficient men to handle it. He delighted in taking off his coat and working alongside the others as he had done in those far off days in St. Albans. *The Graphic* of November 27, 1909, quoted Howard as saying that his father took more interest in seeing a tile for the house nicely adjusted than he did in the biggest engineering undertaking on any of his roads.

For the large shipments of sand, gravel, lumber, and steel, a spur of the Pacific Electric from the Sierra Madre line was routed into the grounds along a gently curving route from San Marino Avenue. A concrete car house was later built at this entrance for the private cars San Marino I and II, where books and art treasures could be unloaded and where the family began their cross-country trips.

Hunt had full control of hiring and coordinating the various contractors, the best available in the United States and Europe. Huntington's original plans were quite austere: "I do not want onyx mantels, but plain, simple mantels. . . . As to the ceiling, I want a very simple plastered cornice." Under Arabella's influence the plans became much more elegant and complex and, although cost was never a factor, Henry Huntington always wanted his money's worth in the finished work.

White, Allom, Ltd., an English firm commissioned through Mrs. Huntington's art dealer, Joseph Duveen, designed the eighteenth-century-French style oak wall paneling in the large library room of the house. The plans were executed in Paris with one of Hunt's superintendents watching and hurrying the work. Thinner woods had to be substituted for those used in European paneling to prevent warping in the dry warm air of Southern California. The original apple-green finish of the dining room showed the influence of mid-eighteenth-century English design, as did the late seventeenth-century style of the woodwork and fireplace in the small office-library room off the porte-cochère. The two drawing rooms were finished in the style of Louis XVI. All in all, $121,284.96 was paid to Duveen Brothers for the White, Allom work. The ornate chandeliers in the library and large drawing room, which reflect *ad infinitum* between the mirrors over the fireplaces of the two rooms, were copies of those at Versailles.

Electricity was supplied by the Pacific Light and Power Company, of which Henry Huntington was a major stockholder. He was reminded of this fact by Arabella when the lights in the whole house once went off during a formal dinner party. The electrical work was done by a clever and independent electrician who, using wire from the Safety Insulated Wire and Cable Company (another Huntington-owned company), developed a wiring system that was entirely new in residential use. When one master switch was pressed, every light in the house would go on, to safeguard the contents from theft and alert the staff if there should be a fire or other emergency. Care was taken to reinforce the second floor against earthquake damage, especially after the experience of the destruction in San Francisco in 1906.

Henry F. Bultitude, who was White, Allom's New York draftsman and designer, was called in to make scale drawings of the rooms and to supervise the decorative plastering. The staircase railing was made in France; the parquet flooring came from New York, as did the plumbing fixtures; the marble work was done in Baltimore. The fireplaces in the downstairs rooms are ornately carved in wood or marble while those in the upstairs bedrooms are of simpler design and conform more to Huntington's original request. Only orangewood from the grounds was burned in the fireplaces. Eucalyptus and oak were used in the furnace, later converted to coal.

When the Beauvais tapestries were purchased by Arabella in Henry Huntington's name, the completed wood moldings for the library room had to be recut and many bookshelves eliminated. The room shows off the four largest of the suite of tapestries to perfection, as there is the necessary space to take in all the details of workmanship and rococo design. Although the wool and silk yarns have faded, it is possible to see the areas where the royal arms of Louis XV had been cut out and rewoven when the tapestries were auctioned off after the French Revolution. The fifth hanging just fits inside the loggia door, which serves today as the main entry for museum visitors. Here it is possible to come close enough to see the signature of the designer, "F. Boucher 1756," woven in reverse in the lower corner.

The library room, despite its size, became the downstairs sitting room of the house and was furnished differently from the way it is today, with a grand piano, a large oak desk, an eight tube "radiola 30," card tables, comfortable chairs, a Scotch rug, a sixteenth-century Persian rug, and potted palms in decorative Chinese containers.

Now the library room is arranged with ten tapestry-covered French chairs and two settees, the backs depicting children and putti engaged in the arts and set into nineteenth-century frames. Five of the stiff tapestry seats are after Oudry's animal illustrations for *The Fables of Fontaine*. All the coverings were executed at the Gobelin Factory, possibly for Madame de Pompadour. These furnishings had previously been divided among the two formal drawing rooms, with a Savonnerie rug from the reign of Louis XIV (now in the library room) adding to the elegance of each.

The interiors of the upstairs rooms and drawing rooms were painted white with a minimum of six coats, usually eight, and sometimes ten, each sanded between applications, the walls finally rubbed smooth with pumice and rottenstone for a satin-like finish. The rooms to the south had a slightly grayish tinge while those to the north had a creamier tone for warmth. Upstairs there were two large, sunny sitting rooms, one off the Huntingtons' bedroom and another closer to the guest wing. There were six bedrooms, six baths, and accommodations for the women servants. Over the staircase railings hung four rare and colorful rugs, one woven with gold and silver threads.

The northeast portion of the basement was built as a commodious wine cellar. It was filled at first with barrels of zinfandel, sherry, port, and sauternes from the San Gabriel Winery, which Huntington had acquired along with the tract of land in Alhambra on which it was situated. The finest imported wines were shipped in when the house began to be lived in. In the estate appraisal of 1927, the contents of this cellar room were assessed at $5,248.83 wholesale, and included eighteen cases of choice champagnes, eighteen cases of brandies, and many wines and whiskies—all listed as medicinal, since this was during Prohibition. Henry Huntington and Arabella used the spirits sparingly; they were meant for entertaining.

Even though the reinforced concrete work on the structure took longer than usual due to rainy weather and delivery delays, the exterior of the house was completed in just fifty-one weeks of work. When asked if it were out of the ordinary for a dwelling of this size and importance to be finished in under a year, Mr. Hunt answered, "I attribute that to the fact that he [Huntington] knew how to get work out of us and he concluded decisions suddenly and very deliberately [and] having once made a decision, he did not swerve from it. He let us employ the best people. Anything he was assured was the best, he felt he could afford." The cost of the house came to just under half a million dollars including White, Allom's work, with another fifty thousand added for the garage, stables, and private railroad car house.

On February 5, 1910, one of the weekly reports east to Huntington from the Huntington Land & Improvement Company on the progress of the house concluded with the following paragraph: "I have your letter with reference to the flag-pole at Redondo, and have been down to see how will be the best way to get it moved to the ranch. It is a very beautiful pole." At that time, and perhaps still, it was the tallest wooden pole in the state and measured 132 feet from the ground up with another 16 feet sunk below the surface—a single Douglas fir from Oregon. It had been sent down the coast to Southern California on a lumber ship, and it was transported between two horsedrawn wagons through the streets to the San Marino Ranch. There it was laboriously installed to the west of the house through the use of a block and tackle and under the supervision of William Hertrich, Ranch superintendent. Now the pole resembles aluminum as it is covered with a silver-colored paint to protect the wood from rotting. The American flag is raised and lowered daily by one of the Art Gallery custodians.

The original schedule had set the date of occupancy for 1911, when the household equipment was installed, some of the art objects in place, and the Japanese garden completed in the old west reservoir. Everything was in order well in advance of Arabella's first visit in January 1914, six months after the Paris wedding. Hertrich met them at the Santa Fé depot in Pasadena. All advance notice was hushed due to Arabella's desire for privacy, but an alert press was waiting with photographers; the family henceforth disembarked at an earlier stop, to be met by car and whisked off in secrecy to the Ranch. Otheman Stevens, Huntington's one trusted journalist friend, went over the first evening looking for a story and said he had never seen Huntington so radiant and did not disturb the couple. One can imagine Huntington's joy in showing off the mansion and grounds to the woman he loved.

Arabella liked everything about the house, with one small exception. The terrace facing south over the San Gabriel Valley, the loggia, and the north portico were laid with square red tiles imported from Wales. She thought the white grout used between them made the areas look like giant checkerboards and so the material was colored to give a more uniform appearance. There was another objection from the servants, that the butler's pantry was located too far away from the door so that when the bell rang it was necessary for the man to race through two halls to answer it. The pantry and the rest of the kitchen and service wing were torn down in 1933 and the north passage (with the collection of miniatures and old silver) and the main exhibition hall of British paintings erected in its place the following year. The maids' rooms in the attic also proved unsatisfactory as they were unbearably hot, so a six-bedroom cottage was finished for them north of the house. The original attic, now remodeled, is part of the art reference library and is reached by a steep circular staircase.

The loggia was a large, attractive outside living space furnished with a marble table, some cold and uncomfortable marble benches, wooden swings that were suspended by hooks from the ceiling, wicker furniture, and many potted palms. Max Gschwind, one of the early grounds foremen, remembered seeing Huntington and Patton seated in a pair of cane chairs playing cards together. Instead of poker chips, a small canyon adjoining their two properties served as stakes, continuing to change hands as they played. Above the loggia was a roof garden that could be reached through Arabella's dressing room. Flowering trees in large tubs enhanced the view from the room, besides softening the glare and heat from the morning sun. Her every pleasure was taken into consideration to lengthen the Ranch visits, for when Arabella was upset or uncomfortable, the staff would get the word to start packing for the family's return to New York.

The massive entrance gates to the grounds came from Beddington Manor, built in 1714 by Sir Nicholas Carew. Henry Huntington bought them in Berkshire, England, on his first trip abroad in 1913. These gates are to the original entrance on Euston Road, now permanently closed to the public. Carloads of garden statuary, benches, and fountains were shipped in to beautify the grounds. Soon Hunt was notified to submit plans for a bungalow or guest house, primarily for the use of Mrs. Huntington's son Archer, and the seldom-used bowling alley and billiard room was completed to the west of the house. It was intended as a masculine retreat and decorated with various animal heads and a stuffed white peacock, and is now a cafeteria.

It would have made an ideal playhouse for the Huntington grandchildren. Clara Huntington, the eldest daughter, was resentful all her life that her children never entered the house during their childhoods. Nor did the Metcalf boys often enjoy the rolling lawns and the great hide-and-seek possibilities of the gardens. There was always bitterness concerning the divorce and it was not until after their own mother's death in 1916 and Arabella's death eight years later that the girls in the family were fully reconciled and spent more time with their father.

Huntington's view of their opposition is revealed in a letter written to Elizabeth on September 2, 1913, from the Hotel Bristol in Paris: "My darling daughter—I have received your letter of the 12th and am surprised and pained and grieved at the language 'If your wife daddy is a sensible woman she cannot expect us to be friendly and the sooner you realize that the easier and better for us all.' This is very strange language to come to me from you who has furnished you with every comfort in the world and who has never had a thought that has not been a loving one I regret more than I can tell you. That you should have that feeling but you certainly never expect any treatment from me that is not the same as you treat my wife She does everything in the world to make me happy and I never dreamed that such happiness could be and I cannot understand why you should be so cruel especially to one who has never had anything but kindly thoughts of you she has always spoken of you kindly Your affectionate Father."

Howard Huntington's family did not have the same viewpoint; they lived close by, and came frequently to the Ranch. One of Howard's daughters remembers the excitement of being allowed to spend the night after her father's redwood shingled house was partially destroyed by fire, and of being escorted into dinner on the arm of Mr. Hapgood, the secretary.

Dinner was always formal. Arabella walked down the hall, hand in hand with her husband and "dressed like a queen" in all her jewelry. Two butlers and two liveried footmen were in attendance. After dinner, coffee was served in the large drawing room where *The Blue Boy* was hung. The household was on a strict time schedule, a leftover from railroad punctuality, with breakfast in the mornings at 9:00 and dinner promptly at 7:00. Family meals were bland in consideration of the Huntingtons' health, with poultry usually the main course. Of this there was a large variety, pheasants, geese, squab, guinea hens, turkeys, and ducks, all raised on the grounds and demanding the full-time attention of one man. The oversupply of eggs was traded to the Model Grocery in Pasadena or sold to the workmen on the place. A small herd of Guernsey cows provided milk, cream, and butter. Winter vegetables and melons were grown in six small greenhouses. Mrs. Huntington wanted all such produce grown on the Ranch even though Hertrich estimated that the cost of each melon came to $2.00 and hothouse tomatoes were $1.00 a pound. When they were not in residence, Ranch produce was sent east via Wells Fargo, of which Henry Huntington was a director. This included boxes of fruits, vegetables, and nuts, all kinds of preserves, and avocados packed carefully in beds of cornmeal that was later fed to the horses.

Arabella Huntington's first visit to San Marino lasted a little over two months. After that, she and her new husband returned to the east and then sailed for France. While on their European honeymoon they had signed a ten-year lease with Baron de Forest to rent his large country house, Chateau Beauregard, at La Celle-St. Cloud between Paris and Versailles. The chateau, now destroyed, had been built by a mistress of Napoleon III on the ruins of a seventeenth-century villa. There were four hundred acres of park and farmland, and a huge aviary, all surrounded by a formidable crenelated wall. It was necessary for Huntington to spend over $100,000 in remodeling the chateau, painting the exterior and interior, modernizing four existing bathrooms, and adding two more baths and a septic tank. The waste had previously been gathered in the basement where it was shoveled out once a week. Twenty-five servants were hired, horses bought for riding and farm work, and mowers, plows, rakes, and an apple crusher for cider acquired.

There was obviously a tacit understanding between Arabella and Henry Huntington that if she endured the isolation and climate of San Marino for a few months a year, he would be expected to spend an equal time abroad. Here he too was isolated, as he did not speak or write or read in French and was far from the things that interested him the most. He wrote wistfully in August 1914, a few months after they had left San Marino, "I don't know when we shall return but I wish I were back now. The shops are opening up in Paris but I seldom go in."

Arabella's delight came from the jewelry and antique stores in Paris. She enjoyed the visits of Collis's foster-daughter, the Princess Clara Hatzfeldt, with whom she always remained friendly even after the dispute over the inheritance, and even more so those of her precious son Archer, whom she never saw in California, despite repeated invitations. The carefree social life of Europe at the time, when wealthy Americans mingled freely with the drifting British and Continental nobility and with artists, actors, musicians, and authors from all over the western world, was a welcome change from the rigid New York society, which had absolutely no interest for her husbands, and which was then unforgiving of new money and dubious genealogy.

The charm of Beauregard lessened in the early 1920s. Servants were hard to find after the war and Archer's trips there came to an end after he became interested in and then married Anna Hyatt, the talented and dedicated American sculptress. Because of Anna's poor health and the pressures of her work, and perhaps the competition between the two women, visits ceased. It was decided to give up the chateau at the conclusion of the lease, and Arabella bade a tearful farewell to the staff. All in all, including a hiatus during World War I, only seven months out of ten years were spent at the chateau. It was closed in October 1923, leaving Huntington with an angry baron who, in a ridiculous manner, wanted his property replaced exactly as it had been at the start of the Huntington occupancy. Eventually he was persuaded to accept the improvements and Joseph Duveen lent his services in disposing of some of the furnishings and equipment, sending the rest to America.

Although there was one last train trip to California in the spring of 1924 when her portrait was painted, Arabella took to her bed upon the return to New York. During the last illness she wanted Archer by her side at all times but it was Henry Huntington who kept the vigil in her room throughout the hot, humid summer, as she sank into an irreversible coma. When she died September 14, 1924, there was no lengthy eulogy in the newspapers, very few letters, no details of her early life, and no authorized biography written except for a commissioned pamphlet which contains scant information on this fascinating woman.

Arabella   IV

"Bell is so good and kind to me and I know she will make my life a very happy one."

Henry E. Huntington, July 13, 1913

In 1850—or was it 1851? or even '49?—a baby girl was born to a family named Yarrington in Richmond, Virginia—or was it down in Union Springs, Alabama? The date and place remain vague as the records were lost in the fires of the Civil War, or possibly even deliberately destroyed. The architectural historian, James Maher, has written in *The Twilight of Splendor* that the baby's father worked with his hands as a machinist or carpenter and died young, leaving his widow Catherine with a houseful of children whom she supported by taking in boarders. The names of the five children are listed in an 1860 Richmond census, including Caroline B. Yarrington, age nine. The most probable conclusion is that this young girl, always noted for her spirit and urge for self-improvement, changed her name to the more fashionable Belle Duval Yarrington, the middle name evidently borrowed from her brother, John Duval Yarrington, who in turn had been named, according to family lore, for an earlier Duval, the first territorial governor of Florida. It was not until much later, influenced by the art dealer Sir Joseph Duveen, that she adopted the more refined "Arabella." On deeds executed in the late 1870s and early '80s, she went by the name Belle D. Y. Worsham. To Collis and Henry Huntington, she was always Belle or Bell. Throughout her life she carried the reputation of being poised, proud, and unpredictable.

Visitors to the Huntington Library know Arabella through the large portrait painted by Sir Oswald Birley in the spring of 1924, which can be seen in the Library building. It shows a formidable person dressed entirely in black and seated in a fine tapestry-covered French chair that is still part of the Huntington collection. Here is an elderly woman who is not afraid to look her age, who has not even bothered to remove her glasses: Henry Huntington called the portrait "an admirable likeness." The black might be mourning for her previous husband, Collis Huntington, but was probably the usual becoming, practical, subdued, but elegant dress that ladies of her age and position were accustomed to wear at that time. The veil and hat were to protect the eyes and complexion from the harsh California sunlight. A family member recalled her in white in the mornings on the Ranch, but obviously she didn't consider that suitable for her portrait any more than the flattering light evening dress that was generally worn in such portraits and that the artist had originally planned. "Scratch that out," she demanded when a preliminary sketch attempted a more youthful pose. She was a remarkable woman and by then, just before her death, she had no need for pretense. At the close of an eventful life, she had every material dream fulfilled.

There is another portrait by an unknown artist of Arabella at eighteen or nineteen years of age, showing a young woman of great beauty. It is probable that she first attracted Collis Huntington's attention at this time, for business took him the first two weeks of July 1869 to White Sulphur Springs, West Virginia, then as now a fashionable resort. Afterwards he went to Richmond, where he seems to have stayed at the Yarrington rooming house. By 1871, Arabella and her mother were living on Lexington Avenue in New York, in a house owned by Collis Huntington and not far from the Huntingtons' own residence at 65 Park Avenue. Arabella is said by relatives of Collis's wife, Elizabeth, to have worked there as a seamstress for a short while. There had earlier been, perhaps, a brief undocumented marriage to a faro banker named John Milton Worsham who already had a wife in Richmond. On November 13, 1905, Henry Huntington's daughter, Elizabeth, wrote to her fiancé John Brockway Metcalf: "She is dear—know you will like her— and bright. She was married the first time when she was fourteen that seems so young doesn't it?"

A son was born on March 10, 1870, named Archer Milton Worsham. Arabella went to Texas for the birth or soon afterwards and stayed with the family of a cotton broker. Years later, the daughter of this family, Miss Caroline Campbell, became Arabella's companion and lived as a member of the Huntington household.

With Collis Huntington's roundabout help, Arabella's next move was to East Fifty-fourth Street in New York City and finally to the other side of Fifth Avenue at 4 West Fifty-fourth Street. This was a fine property and soon became larger still with the purchase of two adjoining lots, all told worth $331,000. The house was unpretentious, of ordinary brick with a facing of brownstone along the front. There were many large shade trees, a stable, and a garden to the side with a gazebo. With the help of an architect, Arabella, for the first time, was able to indulge her talent in decorating. The interior was stripped down and completely redecorated with new wallcoverings, draperies, and furnishings. An Otis elevator was installed, one of the first in a private residence. We may get a glimpse of three of these rooms for, when Arabella finally moved, she took nothing but her clothes, and the heirs of the next owners, the John D. Rockefellers, bequeathed them to two museums. The exotic Moorish parlor is shown at the Brooklyn Museum and the dressing room and bedroom with its huge canopied sleigh bed and fall-front desk, containing a secret velvet-lined compartment for jewels, are on display at the Museum of the City of New York. The style of the furniture is predominantly late Victorian, although less ponderous and fussy than most pieces of the period—a credit to Arabella's innate good taste. The site of the house later became the garden of the Museum of Modern Art.

Collis Huntington had been married at age twenty-three to Elizabeth Stoddard, a year or two older and a distant relative. She was a sweet, gentle woman, uncomplaining of the early hardships when her handsome, industrious husband was in the hardware business in Sacramento during the gold-rush years, of her own backbreaking work cooking and caring for his clerks and clients, and of the later loneliness when he was often away on railroad business. Collis longed for a son but it was not until after Elizabeth's brother-in-law died of injuries sustained in a flood that a child, Clara, came into their household. In 1883, Elizabeth died of cervical cancer in New York, at the Park Avenue house.

The following July, in 1884, Arabella married Collis Huntington who, by now, controlled railroads extending from the Atlantic to the Pacific. The ceremony was performed, for a gratuity of four one-thousand dollar bills, by Henry Ward Beecher, the flamboyant religious leader and the brother of novelist Harriet Beecher Stowe. Collis was sixty-three and his bride approximately thirty-four. It was a small wedding with only Arabella's family present, including her mother, Catherine Yarrington, who had served these many years as chaperone to the increasingly wealthy "widow Worsham"; her brother, John Duval Yarrington, who had been employed by Collis Huntington for twelve years; and her teenage son Archer, who then took the Huntington name. After his mother's death, Archer went to great pains to establish that he was Collis's son but his paternity was never officially confirmed.

There are no details known about the honeymoon but the newlyweds might have gone directly to their 113-acre estate at Throgg's Neck overlooking Long Island Sound, recently purchased from Henry Havemeyer. This was to become their legal residence but not their principal home for, within a few years, building plans were being studied for a grand mansion at the corner of Fifth Avenue and Fifty-seventh Street, New York

City, on the site now occupied by Tiffany & Company, the well-known jewelers. Their first choice of architect was Richard Morris Hunt, famous for mansions commissioned by the very wealthy, but since he was unavailable one of his pupils, George Post, took the job. Post turned out a large ugly edifice of uncertain style, with a domed inner courtyard in the center surrounded by marble balconies and pillars, a white and gold Louis XV drawing room, and a dining room hung with Gobelin tapestries. The decorations included some handsome murals on canvas by Elihu Vedder and other contemporary artists of note, gradually augmented as the Huntingtons traveled and frequented the New York auctions. Arabella's bathroom was described as the most splendid in the world, the bath a plunge of running water scented by a constant spray of cologne. The flooring of the room was white marble set with strips of blue tile and there was a path around the tub inset with Turkish rugs. A bank of flowers and palms completed the decor.

Soon Collis Huntington, who earlier boasted that he never spent more than two hundred dollars a year on himself and hired a Chinese cook instead of a fashionable French chef, became involved in accumulating a collection of eighteenth- and nineteenth-century paintings. When Alva Vanderbilt, the socially ambitious wife of William Kissam Vanderbilt, began raising funds for the new uptown Metropolitan Opera House to rival the established Academy of Music on Fourteenth Street, the Huntingtons subscribed magnificently enough to assure a box in the prestigious Diamond Horseshoe. But Arabella's dreams of social triumphs in the imposing Fifth Avenue palace were never fulfilled.

Rumor had it that her husband (whom she always called Mr. Huntington or Papa) was highly uncomfortable in all the city grandeur. For a six-foot-four giant of a man, the antique beds were too short and the delicate chairs broke whenever he sat in them. A resourceful furniture maker was called in to provide a massive upholstered chair that could be adjusted to different positions by a complicated system of levers. Collis refused to be dominated by Arabella, who must have shuddered at the contraption amid her elegant surroundings.

Not long before his death, Collis wrote of selling the mansion and spending his winters in San Francisco, thus retracting his earlier edict that the California climate was just for sissies. He was happiest in the least elaborate of his homes, Pine Knot Lodge in the Adirondack Mountains. The main rooms were comfortable but rustic, while the dozen bathrooms were magnificent in marble with elaborate brass fixtures. It was here in August 1900 that Collis Huntington suddenly died, a shock to his family and to the world of finance.

In his lengthy, complicated will, the New York town house was left to Arabella for her lifetime, then to Archer, after which, if Archer were childless, it was to go to Yale University. This is where the Vedder murals from the house may be seen today, removed before it was demolished. (Elihu Vedder's 1879 painting, *The Dying Sea Gull,* is one of the American canvases shown in the Virginia Steele Scott Gallery on the Huntington grounds.) In addition to other considerations, $500,000 was left in trust to Arabella, $250,000 to Archer, and $1,000,000 to Clara for her personal use.

The newspapers called Arabella the richest woman in the world after Collis's death. Later she would regale Howard's daughters with funny anecdotes of the many suitors attracted by her inheritance. Arabella was capable of managing her own business affairs and kept her accounts strictly separate from those of Henry Huntington after their marriage. She was credited with "a forceful, dominating intellect," could converse knowledgeably with her lawyers and realtors, and give sound economic advice. She was tall, restless, and an insatiable reader despite the poor eyesight brought on by an early bicycle accident or perhaps by the use of belladonna which was, in those days, often used as a cosmetic for adding sparkle to the eyes.

There are few of Arabella's letters available for research. Those written to Archer were destroyed by the Hispanic Society in New York. Others concerning the divorce were burned by Caroline Holladay following her brother's death. The handful remaining are difficult to decipher as Arabella's poor eyesight translated into erratic penmanship. But, although outsiders could consider her difficult, distant, and demi-mondaine, the preserved correspondence shows a caring relationship with those dearest to her.

For many years, she had made the education of young Archer her main interest and, as he learned history and the classics, she also learned. She spoke French fluently and became knowledgeable in French history and the decorative arts. There was an unusually strong bond between mother and son. Archer never attended school or college but went on to become a well-known scholar, connoisseur of the arts, and the founder of the Hispanic Society in New York. His letters were elaborately witty and his talk described as "like summer lightning." Arabella customarily gave her son on his birthday a thousand dollars for every year of his life and never returned from a shopping tour without an expensive present for him. In 1900 she gave property at Broadway and 156th Street in New York to the American Geographical Society, of which he was president. In 1910 she paid $400,000 for Velasquez's portrait *The Duke of Olivares* and donated it to his Hispanic Society. Archer was always her special pride.

Clara admired her Aunt Belle and copied her in spirit and independence. When she married the German prince, she brought in her dowry "magnificent settlements and superb jewels." Clara's husband, Prince François-Edmond-Joseph-Gabriel Vit de Hatzfeldt Wildenbourg, was the son of the German ambassador to Britain. Collis was firmly opposed to the wedding as the prince's main attributes, a title and perfect manners, were not among those he considered important in a son-in-law. Arabella and Clara joined together to over-rule him. There was visiting back and forth among the families but Clara and her prince preferred living abroad at their English country estate, Foliejon Park, near Windsor. They had no children.

The years after Collis's death were spent in frequent trips to Paris, where Arabella went on a glorious spending spree of unprecedented proportions. She spent lavishly, constantly, and incredibly on pearls and porcelains, furnishings and figurines, clocks and candelabra. In 1908 she also bought the Hotel de Hirsch, on the Rue de l'Elysée, an elegant home that had once belonged to the Empress Eugènie, which contained a monumental marble staircase, a large winter garden, and boiseries from the Chateau de Bercy. It was reported she paid $300,000 for the house and spent over $100,000 in renovations, including fourteen bathrooms to replace a single tin tub.

Helping her in this project was Sir Joseph Duveen, who treated her as one of his special clients, an unusual and calculated compliment as Duveen was famous for his selectivity. He would work only with patrons who could appreciate the very best and thought it a privilege to pay for it. His opinions were absolute and unarguable and his method of instruction completely one-sided; he did all the talking, constantly and contagiously. He loved walking through the galleries or window shopping along the great boulevards with one of his wealthy disciples, giving the awed pupil the exciting sense of being involved in an unforgettable experience. He was a shrewd master of artistic tutoring, flattery, and psychology, a man of enormous vigor and audacity, and it was largely owing to his influence that American taste in art was transformed in the early years of this century.

The Hotel de Hirsch was sold just nineteen months after its purchase, probably because of Arabella's coming marriage to Henry Huntington and her concentration on the house that was being designed for them by Myron Hunt on the San Marino Ranch. One can see how her ideas evolved and were refined by comparing this house with her New York houses, the Paris Hotel, Chateau Beauregard, and the dignified structure atop Nob Hill that Collis had bought for her in 1892, built by a railroad associate, David Colton. Its facade of wood, cut and painted to look like stone, was remarkably free from the towers, bays, and jigsaw gingerbread that decorated the other magnates' ostentatious homes nearby. After the 1906 earthquake and fire, the site of this house, with its sensational view of the harbor and hills beyond, was presented by Arabella to the city of San Francisco to be used as a children's park and playground.

Never again, after living in Paris, would Arabella accept anything but the best in architecture and decoration. She was consulted on all the preliminary plans for the house in San Marino and, with Duveen, suggested the great portraits and tapestries to fill the rooms.

"Belle, as you know, is exceedingly particular," Collis Huntington had written to his nephew in 1896. She was a perfectionist when it came to the construction and furnishings of the San Marino house. She admired *The Blue Boy* very much, loved Raeburn's *Master Blair* best of all because the eyes reminded her of Archer, but was shocked with the idea of hanging a portrait of an actress in her home. It took all of Duveen's vast persuasive powers to convince her—"It is the artist that matters—not the subject"—before Reynolds's *Sarah Siddons* could be sent to California.

Henry Huntington and Arabella were married, after years of postponements on her part, on July 16, 1913, at the American Church in Paris. She continued to wear Collis's wedding band together with her new ring on the same hand for the rest of her life. Let Henry Huntington tell us about it in a letter written to his younger sister Carrie, a few weeks later from Lausanne. "How quickly the years do pass and yet how slow when we are waiting for the most cherished things to come to us. But now, my dear sister, all that I hoped for has come to me, and Belle and I are so very happy. She never seemed so free of care and responsibility and looks years younger. . . . [We] expect to go to California soon after the first of the year but it may be before that when we hope to see you in our new home. The word home to one who has had none for a long time is so inexpressibly sweet and now it seems I am just beginning to live and life seems so very, very sweet." His devotion never diminished and the rest of his life was spent contentedly in love with his adored Belle.

The Huntingtons arrived in San Marino the winter of 1914 to find everything in readiness, but after ten weeks they returned to Chateau Beauregard. It was Henry's greatest pleasure to be at his California Eden but the summer heat bothered Arabella and she always missed Archer, for he never visited, even after becoming one of the original Library trustees in 1919. In New York he customarily took lunch every day with his mother at the Fifty-seventh Street home and was best known to the servants for his capacity for caviar. Arabella worried about him constantly and treated him as a small boy. She asked William Hertrich, Ranch superintendent, to find a ten-acre orange grove to entice her son west. She finally bought for him the Old Mill property, later given to the widow of Henry Huntington's son Howard, with the provision that the premises should eventually become a historical monument.

Arabella ordered her clothes from Paris and often the arrival of the couturier in New York delayed the trips to California as countless fittings were necessary. Aside from the famous art collections, she loved and could appreciate fine laces, fans, and other textiles. In the inventory of the San Marino house in 1927, one upstairs linen closet alone was described as crammed with altar cloths, Chinese tapestries, velvets, brocades, and embroidered kimonos. One can only imagine what treasures the New York town house yielded after her death.

The Huntingtons seldom entertained with large gatherings, preferring card games or occasional musical evenings with Miss Campbell at the piano. Collis Holladay, Carrie's son, reported that his Aunt Belle played a beautiful game of bridge, holding the cards very close to her eyes. Croquet was a daytime recreation and there were the birdcages to be visited with their tame and colorful occupants, probably similar to the great aviary at Beauregard, and the housedogs to be spoiled.

In the house lived a parrot with a large vocabulary who could mimic Arabella's voice to perfection. One of its phrases repeated over and over again was "Edward, hurry up! Come up here! Go to bed!" Arabella loved all animals and they were also always fond of her. One little dog, Buster, was mauled by a watchdog on the grounds. She would walk out in the afternoons at five to lay a single flower on the grave.

Guests were usually family members or business associates including, of course, Duveen, charming and indispensable and always accompanied by good cheer and the crates and cartons that made his trips west seem like Christmas. In 1920 the Library building was approaching completion and the book collection was moved from New York. The elegant, erudite Dr. A. S. W. Rosenbach, who was selling incunables and rare books and manuscripts to Mr. Huntington, occasionally dealt also with Arabella, who was eager to share her husband's interests. Rosenbach was a frequent visitor to San Marino and often brought with him the lavishly illustrated and intricately bound volumes she enjoyed buying.

Arabella died in her home in New York City on September 14, 1924, after an illness of two months. Although many of her letters refer to lameness, terrible colds, neuralgia, stomach upsets, and unspecified disorders, her personality was so powerful that it suggested a strong constitution; Clara Hatzfeldt wrote from England, "with her wonderful vitality, I cannot but feel she will pull through." But after a siege of high fever and transfusions, an operation was performed for an abscess on the kidney and she rapidly declined.

A funeral service was held at the Fifty-seventh Street house in New York. Out of respect, all the streetcars and buses of the Los Angeles Railway, of which Henry Huntington was president, were halted for one minute at 12:00 noon, September 18, the time corresponding to that of the funeral. The body was returned by private car to San Marino where another service, attended only by a few, was held, conducted by the minister of the Presbyterian Church of Pasadena. The casket was then taken near the site she had selected for the mausoleum and temporarily encased in a cement vault until the marble tomb could be completed. The date and place of birth later carved on the mausoleum were supplied by Archer at Henry's request; her past had never concerned him. A special permit from the County Board of Supervisors was necessary, to allow for an interment in private property.

In her will were legacies to relatives, servants, and a few institutions; her estate was valued at $17,516,747. Everything else went to Archer and, with this inheritance and with no children of his own, he was generous to literary, scientific, and artistic institutions across the country. He established museums throughout the eastern states and in Spain and is quoted as saying, "Wherever I put my foot down, a museum springs up." One of the most famous is the Hispanic Society in New York City, built on land that was earlier owned by John James Audubon, and another is Brookgreen Gardens in South Carolina, the ten-thousand-acre plantation and sculpture garden. Other museums are the Mariners at Newport News, Virginia, and one in Seville, Spain. He established a series of wild life forest stations along the eastern seaboard and even a golf museum at the James River Country Club near Newport News.

To honor the woman he loved, Henry Huntington had red Genoese velvet wall coverings (since replaced) brought out from the New York house. They served as a backdrop for the collection of Renaissance furniture and paintings which make up the north room of the Arabella Huntington Memorial Collection in the Library. The collection had been acquired from Archer, and Duveen helped choose the French furniture, sculpture, and Sèvres porcelains also displayed in galleries of the wing.

In the estate appraisal is a typewritten sheet of fourteen pages with a description and valuation of Arabella's jewelry, which was inherited by Archer. The combined worth of the 121 pieces was $1,274,904. The report describes a trove of pearls, diamonds, and other precious stones: items varied from a diamond-studded hatpin valued at $35 to the rope of 160 Oriental pearls, weighing 2,156 grams, with a double diamond clasp, which had an estimated value of $444,126. This strand was put together one by one, year by year, so that each pearl matched the others in size and shading. It had to be divided into thirds to be sold, as the entire necklace was too precious for any individual to afford. There were seven other pearl necklaces, including one of black pearls with small rose diamond rondels between each pearl. Emeralds seem to have been preferred to other precious stones and, surprisingly, between the sunbursts, crescents, bowknots, and clusters, there are three frog-shaped brooches of differing designs that must have had a special significance. Collis's first important purchase for her had been a glittering rope of 119 blue diamonds from Tiffany. After Collis's death, Arabella, with ample funds to satisfy any desire, had become a compulsive buyer of the beautiful things that most attracted her. Remembering the early days in Richmond, she might have also treasured the jewelry as security against ever being poor again.

Arabella is often shown wearing pearls in her portraits—a woman who rose above her humble beginnings, who braved the envy of others, who educated both herself and her son, who helped and delighted two famous men, and who has left us with a heritage of immense value. For without her guiding hand, it is doubtful that the great treasures of the Huntington art collection would have been gathered together, to bring enjoyment and instruction to those thousands of visitors who view them each year.

The Art Collection   V

"You have the greatest collection of English pictures which exists,
and every great one you add to it is worth more to you than anyone
else."
                           Joseph Duveen to Henry Huntington, August 9, 1915

Joseph Duveen, art dealer extraordinary, concentrated for five
decades on the joys and profits of marketing paintings, furniture, objets d'art, and himself to the new American millionaires. His clients had largely come from hardworking, middle-
class families who had only lately awakened to the realization
that there was more to life than amassing dollars. They wanted
to decorate their mansions with the treasures of earlier eras
and to leave something behind as memorials to themselves.
They had also discovered the competition of collecting and the
international prestige of purchasing important paintings.
However, the art markets were largely a mystery and so they
eagerly turned to the man whose effervescence, artistic background, and adroit psychology taught them to become, if not
connoisseurs, at least proud of their new possessions.

 Duveen has sometimes been criticized for his clever ma-
nipulation of buyers, sellers, and even scholars but he has left,
indirectly, a legacy to the American people. He deserves credit
for helping to arouse a provincial country to an appreciation of
the Old Masters shown in appropriate settings. Without his
drive and determination, a large proportion of the holdings
now in museums on both coasts of America could never have

been sought out in Great Britain and in Europe, authenticated, and packed for transatlantic shipment.

Duveen became friend and confidant to his clients and was able to make himself indispensable. A compulsive worker, he traveled constantly between offices in London, Paris, and New York, seeking contacts to buy and to sell. His brother-in-law, art dealer René Gimpel, tells in his diary of a harassed employee's complaint that it was lunch time and Duveen's sharp rejoinder that when he was young, he ate lunch only on Sundays. His *modus operandi* becomes apparent in his eighteen-year correspondence with Henry Huntington, whose acquisitions from Duveen form the nucleus of the collection in the Huntington Art Gallery.

Joseph Duveen was one of a large family of Dutch origin which had settled in London. His father, Sir Joseph Joel Duveen, was a prosperous purveyor of fine furniture, tapestries, and porcelains with a keen eye for decorative detail. One of his favored clients in the late nineteenth century was the eldest son of Queen Victoria, who from time to time would drop in at Duveen's Oxford Street shop. When the prince succeeded to the throne as Edward VII in 1901, the senior Duveen was knighted for having arranged much of the coronation ceremony at Westminster Abbey by supplying decorative carpets, tapestries, and a pair of specially designed thrones. It was taken for granted that young Joseph, the eldest son, should learn the family business. In an undated document in the Huntington archives, he wrote of a profitable day of instruction:

"Some twenty years ago, Lady Henry Somerset wrote to my Father (the late Sir Joseph Duveen), informing him that she had some tapestry overdoors for sale, and that she would like him to come to Eastnor Castle, Malvern, on the West Coast of England, to see her in regard to them. I accompanied my Father there, and in due time, the question of the overdoors was being discussed by her Ladyship, my father was endeavoring to obtain the overdoors at a lower price, and during the conversation at this point, I left the room and wandered along the corridors of the Castle. Being (in those days), a very inquisitive person, I opened one of the large doors leading from a long corridor, and was surprised to find myself in an enormous room, painted in white, with large panels, from which it was very evident to my mind that tapestries at one time formed the chief decoration of the room, and had been taken down. Surmising that probably the tapestries had been removed for sale, or possibly had been sold, I returned to the room where my Father and her Ladyship were still discussing the overdoors, and in an interval of conversation, inquired whether there were not other tapestries, viz:—those which were hung in the room I just left. Her Ladyship smilingly asked me how I knew she had possessed other tapestries, and I told her of my visit to the large Salon. She then informed us that she had possessed other tapestries, but she sold them the year before to Mr. Kann of Paris. My Father, being naturally very interested, asked her Ladyship what kind of tapestries they were, and she told us that they were a set of five Boucher panels, the finest in existence.

After a lapse of about ten years, we made the acquaintance of Mr. Rudolphe Kann of Paris, and he kindly showed us his collection, where for the first time, we saw the celebrated Boucher set and at the same time, upon hearing which, he remarked to my Father, 'Well, Duveen, you will never get them now.' Mr. Kann dies, and to the surprise of everybody in France, the Collection was not left to the Louvre, as anticipated. The Collection was left to his three sisters and one brother, and for the purposes of division, had to be sold. My father was always much more interested in the tapestries than in any other items.

I admit he had more knowledge of tapestries than of anything else, but it was really through his interests in these panels, and the Rembrandt pictures that we finally made up our minds to buy the Collection. Our object was always to keep the set intact, in fact, I recall a remark made by my Father, 'Boys, there (alluding to the Bouchers) is our savings bank, and you never need be in a hurry to sell them.' I may add that we could have sold the set many times over, had we elected to offer them separately . . . but we were determined to keep them and sell them en bloc."

The younger Duveen first became acquainted with Arabella Huntington in the early years of the century when, now a widow, she was spending much of her time abroad. The introduction was performed by Count Hector Baltazzi, one of the quasi-nobility who frequented Paris and the Continental spas, part of the social set that circulated around the gregarious Princess Clara Hatzfeldt, and it was probably she who introduced him to her Aunt Belle. Duveen Brothers gratefully paid the count a fee of $50,000 as Arabella became entranced with Duveen's courteous manner—she said he always treated her "like a Queen"—and his wondrous wares. Never able to achieve the social prominence she thought commensurate with the Huntington wealth and influence, she compensated by turning her ambitions to the assembling of a collection that became the envy of her contemporaries and made Duveen famous throughout the art world.

The older family members of the firm of Duveen Brothers had been dubious, after the patriarch's death, of the success of the Kann sale. But Joseph Duveen never lacked self-reliance and the collection ultimately realized a large profit. Arabella Huntington spent $2,500,000, to buy most of the furniture and many paintings, including the great Rembrandt *Aristotle Contemplating the Bust of Homer*, which hung in her New York town house until her death and is now at the Metropolitan Museum. The five Boucher tapestries of *The Noble Pastoral*— *The Flute Lesson, The Pleasures of Fishing, The Bird Catchers, The Vintage*, and *Country Pleasures*—woven at Beauvais for Louis XV were reserved at the sale by Arabella. The statement was forwarded to Henry Huntington, then in San Marino decorating his new home. The bill of $577,000 was more than the cost of the entire house and outbuildings. It was Huntington's first major purchase and one that had a special meaning for Arabella. During the San Francisco earthquake and fire a few years earlier, Boucher's *Les Tentures de François Boucher,* a set of four tapestries sold by the senior Joseph Duveen to Collis Huntington about 1880, were destroyed and she was eager to replace them with a finer, rarer suite.

Henry Huntington had previously bought a few unrelated landscapes and portraits from other dealers, but the first note from Duveen Brothers, in June 1909, set the stage for marvelous purchases to come. "Dear Sir: We have received from our London House a number of illustrated catalogues of the Kann Collection which we are instructed to hand to you." Thus it was, through Arabella's early intervention and his own later enthusiasm, that the great Huntington Art Gallery took shape, with Duveen constantly prodding, flattering, and giving freely of advice and services.

Although Henry and Arabella Huntington were not married until 1913, as early as 1906 plans were made for the large house on the knoll overlooking the San Gabriel Valley. After the architectural firm of Myron Hunt & Elmer Grey was engaged, Duveen was consulted on the interior decorations, and he promptly ordered a scale model of the library room. It was Duveen's pleasure and profit to make these small doll-house rooms to give his clients a better idea of proportion and to point out to them the bare walls that needed further embellishment. He charged $25,000 apiece for these models, complete with furniture, mirrors, rugs, chandeliers, and tiny tapestries.

In October 1909, the English firm of White, Allom signed a contract with Duveen Brothers providing interior finish to the residence and the wood paneling in the library room, with special provision made later to accommodate the framed *Noble Pastoral* from the Kann Collection.

Duveen was canny enough to exploit Huntington's competitive drive. In 1911, he wrote, "The other day I was telling Mrs. Huntington that I could remember only one other full-length portrait of a lady by Gainsborough in the whole of America and that was the painting which we sold to Mr. Frick last year."

From then on the Huntingtons concentrated with few exceptions on English portraits, principally of women, from the eighteenth century, which seems to have been Mr. Huntington's preference. Secondary emphasis was given to the French furniture and accessories from the same period, of which Arabella was particularly fond and about which she was knowledgeable. A decision to limit buying to a certain time span was unusual among Duveen's clientele, whose tastes were generally less circumscribed. The resolution imposed limitations on the dealer but has enhanced the glories of the Art Gallery, where the fine collection of English paintings features a harmonious group of full-length portraits dating from about 1700 to 1800.

On July 24, 1911, a cable from Arabella Huntington was received at the Ranch: "Have seen Duveen's purchases Wertheimer Collection—best are three pictures which you must not miss—namely two full Gainsboroughs—Man and Wife—magnificent finest possible price—beautiful woman blue and white dress large black hat slightly restored—answer me immediately A. D. Huntington." The full-length Gainsboroughs were of Lord and Lady Ligonier and the woman in the black hat, *Lady Petre*, the portrait found on Gainsborough's easel when he died in 1788. Henry Huntington was at first apprehensive when Arabella cabled, "Have offered seven hundred and fifty thousand dollars for three full length Gainsboroughs offer refused will you offer more time can be arranged." The cost for the three finally came to $775,000, a huge sum in those days and indicative of the prices Duveen could ask when the very wealthy were scrambling to buy. Duveen wrote Henry Huntington: "The three Gainsboroughs you now own are simply wonderful. No words of mine can do them justice. . . . Mrs. Huntington came in again yesterday, just before leaving for the cure and had a final look at the pictures. She went away quite happy, and said she was so pleased that she had been able to secure them for you."

Even the arrangements for the wedding of Henry and

Arabella Huntington were handled by Duveen, according to S. N. Behrman, as he states in his biography of Duveen. There is nothing in the letters to support this notion, but the information rings true. One of Duveen's great charms was his ability to get things done for his clients, to make life run more smoothly and pleasantly.

During the first few days of World War I, the Huntingtons were caught at Chateau Beauregard, located between Paris and Versailles, unable to leave the country. After hurriedly sending his wife and daughter and their lady's maid off in a taxi to safety, Duveen borrowed the limousine of Sir Austen Lee, the British ambassador, and drove with the Huntingtons to Le Havre, where his gift of persuasion plus the importance of the diplomatic car led to passage on a British ship. Duveen's courageous and generous deed together with his business sense and contagious love of art won the Huntington's lifelong gratitude, to the point where the dealer had virtually a monopoly with them on the buying of great British and European treasures. Some charged that he was a knave who would stoop to any deception in order to complete a sale, but it is obvious that the Huntington relationship was one of mutual esteem.

In a revealing interview taped in 1959, Alphonso Gomez, Mr. Huntington's valet, was asked about Duveen's interest in money. Gomez replied, "I never heard a man talk like Duveen that I think I will sneak anyplace just to listen to him. He was wonderful. But I never saw Mr. Duveen tell Mr. or Mrs. Huntington that he was going to sell them something without telling them how much he was going to make. He told them what he wanted. . . . That was regardless of whether Mrs. Huntington was there, or the servants, he told plain, loud—you could hear him all over the house—what he wanted to make. But he said to Mr. Huntington, 'The reason I want $300,000 for myself is because I want that painting to stay in this house. It doesn't belong to Mr. Rockefeller, it doesn't belong to Mellon; this belongs here and that's why I want you to have it. If you don't want it for the house, then I can make more profit. I won't make $300,000 on that picture, I'll make $500,000 on it.' . . . He proved to Mr. and Mrs. Huntington who wanted that picture and how much more they would give than them. In other words he had vision. He knew which pictures should be here, which should be there. And the same thing happened with *The Blue Boy*. I heard talk about *The Blue Boy* till my head got hot. . . . Mr. Duveen made up his mind that *Pinkie* and *Blue Boy* should be in California . . . and that's why I think that Mr. and Mrs. Huntington were crazy for him. . . . I have a very strong faith that Mr. Duveen didn't make a dollar off Mr. and Mrs. Huntington that they didn't know, because they knew exactly."

About the financial dealings, Duveen himself wrote Henry Huntington: "True, we have our little discussions about prices towards the end of my stay, but then these are merely business talks between one businessman and another and have nothing to do with our mutual friendship. The circumstances are really like those concerning two great barristers—enemies in court but outside their friendship is unimpaired!"

Perhaps it was Huntington's innate honesty and "exhaustless good nature" that brought out the best in Duveen. Perhaps it was the fact that provenances were much clearer for eighteenth-century works than for those of the Italian Renaissance favored by many other American collectors. Or another reason for the compatibility between the two men might have been that Huntington felt about his art dealings as he did about his book purchases. In 1909 he wrote to the Philadelphia dealer, Charles Sessler, "I am glad to say that my dealings with you in books during the last few months have been very satisfactory to me, and I imagine equally so to yourself. The books I purchased from you were what I wanted for my particular purposes, and while, of course, I paid you too much for some, I got a good many at figures quite acceptable to me and I had not the time to go shopping about for better bargains. When I paid you the tall prices, I felt at the time I owed it to you as a tribute to your linguistic ability and your transcendent qualities as a salesman of literary commodities, both of which used to excite my sincere admiration."

After the initial burst of activity, and while the Huntingtons settled into their new winter home, Duveen concentrated on his other customers. But when the J. Pierpont Morgan Collection was sold at auction, the two grand Savonnerie rugs were acquired by the Huntingtons in 1915, and two years later when the Morgan Renaissance bronzes, enamels, and majolicas were bought by Duveen Brothers, Joseph Duveen wrote, "I am, of course, reserving for inspection the fine bronzes."

In 1917, a group of twenty-two of these small Italian, French, and Flemish Renaissance bronzes arrived in San Marino, most of them dating from about 1600. Among the artists is Giovanni Bologna (1529-1608), who is represented by the small classical figure of *Nessus and Deïanira*. Seventeen of the figurines are now displayed on shelves in the small wood-paneled room to the right of the loggia entrance to the Gallery. Others are distributed in the Main Exhibition Hall and in the Library building. Each bronze was meant to be minutely examined and the delicate play of light on the contours and the richness of the patina admired. One can easily see why the Huntingtons yielded to the temptation of purchasing these exquisite statuettes—an acquisition outside the main focus of the collection—much as the beautifully illuminated French and Flemish Books of Hours were added to the predominantly English and American contents of the Library collection.

Duveen's most expensive individual sale to Henry Huntington was Gainsborough's celebrated portrait *The Blue Boy* (c. 1770), without doubt the best-known English painting in the world. This famous oil shows a young family friend of the artist and was planned, in pose, costume, and technique, to honor the work of an earlier artist, Van Dyck, who had painted the English court of Charles I. *The Blue Boy*, which Gainsborough made simply for his own pleasure, was a great public success and led to further major commissioned portraits.

The purchase was arranged in October 1921, when the Huntingtons were staying at their rented chateau outside of Paris. *The Blue Boy* had been in the possession of the Dukes of Westminster for over a hundred years. Edward Fowles, then Duveen's assistant, wrote in his memoirs that after Duveen had acquired the portrait, he had mounted it in a new frame, brightened the varnish, and invited the Huntingtons to come call. Duveen planned the seating carefully and kept up a non-stop stream of conversation, artfully throwing in the price as if it were inconsequential. Arabella fell in love at first sight while Henry Huntington, less impetuous and more businesslike, made an appointment to return alone the next day. Not his usual lighthearted self, he then said not a word but scribbled down a few figures and departed. Duveen was ecstatic; he knew the quiet manner meant a serious buyer.

The following day, Duveen Brothers received a handwritten letter with the agreement to purchase the portrait for the equivalent of $728,000, payable at six-month intervals. Duveen was given the option of exhibiting it before delivery for two weeks at the National Gallery in London, where thousands made a farewell visit, and for another three weeks at the House of Duveen at Fifty-sixth Street and Fifth Avenue in New York. The admission fee charged at the New York showing went for the benefit of charity. Of the exhibition, Duveen wrote, "After much consideration, we decided that Two Dollars would be a fair charge to make for admission, in aid of the Fifth Avenue Hospital Fund, and it appears to have been just the charge to make. We have had an average daily attendance of five or six hundred, composed of the best people in New York and vicinity. The consequence of making such a charge is that we have not been in any way overcrowded and thus enabled to easily handle the number of visitors."

There was at least one other view of the occasion. Jacques Seligmann, the French dealer from whom in 1909 Arabella Huntington had bought (and charged to her prospective bridegroom) the set of Oudry and Boucher chair and settee tapestries, was not among those attending. A bitter rival of Duveen's over a long period of time, nevertheless Seligmann could write Huntington a reassuring letter:

"Your beautiful picture, The Blue Boy, is on Exhibition at Duveen's. I am sorry to say that I cannot go in and look at it because I have no desire to go to Duveen's place. It is a pity that this marvelous work of art was not exhibited at a neutral place. . . . Quite a few people whom I have seen here find that the picture has been cleaned too much, that the cheeks of the boy have been refreshed, that one hand has become nearly invisible, and all kinds of nasty critics [*sic*]. I hope that, when you get the clippings from the papers and read these critics that you won't allow people to disgust you of this beautiful picture."

The last stop in England on *The Blue Boy*'s itinerary had been a visit to the dowager Lady Duveen, widowed mother of Joseph Duveen. Many years earlier the family had made fun of young Joseph's immaturity when he falsely attributed a painting to Gainsborough and he vowed that he would someday have in his possession a great and genuine Gainsborough portrait. All his life, Duveen was plagued by a sense of insecurity despite an outward facade of complete confidence. He was happily married to Elsie Salamon, an acknowledged beauty, the golden-haired, violet-eyed daughter of a moderately wealthy New York tobacco merchant; had an adored daughter, Dorothy; a successful business; and a chance to mingle with the leaders of his world. However, although his father had given his eight sons a good general schooling, college was denied the boys for fear they might become lazy gentlemen. For this reason, Duveen sent his nephew, Armand Lowengard, to Oxford to have the education and advantages he himself had missed. Dorothy attended a fashionable boarding school and Elsie studied voice when her husband was occupied with his clients and dressed always in black and white, fashioned by one of the great European designers, as a perfect background for her elegant surroundings. Duveen wore only new white silk shirts, discarding each at the end of the day and, like British royalty, never carried pocket money, depending on an aide to take care of incidentals.

The Blue Boy left England by a roundabout route and came to San Marino in March 1922. This was Duveen's first trip to California, and his letter to the Huntingtons in preparation was a model of tact and opportunism, "As I am told that the hotels in Los Angeles are rather full, I would feel so much obliged to you if you would kindly help me with a little advice as to the best hotel in which to stay in order that I may telegraph for the necessary reservations."

Subsequently, Duveen made many trips west, always yielding to the Huntingtons' warm invitation to stay at the Ranch, accompanied by his valet and one or two assistants to help in hanging the paintings. In a 1925 interview with the *Pasadena Star News* he said: "This is a divine paradise. I love it better and better, and someday I'm coming here to live . . . among the sunshine and flowers."

The Blue Boy was first hung in the larger of the two formal drawing rooms. Today it is shown in the center of the great exhibition hall and, although it is cloyingly familiar through overexposure in cheap reproductions on candy boxes, calendars, and greeting cards, the power and charm of the original cannot be denied.

On this trip, Duveen brought with him another painting, *Sarah Siddons as the Tragic Muse* (1784) by Sir Joshua Reynolds, first president of the Royal Academy of Arts. Sir Thomas Lawrence, who later became president of the Royal Academy, called it "the finest female portrait in the world." The picture shows the great Shakespearean actress in her costume as Lady Macbeth, sitting on an imposing throne, suggested by Michelangelo's poses of the prophets in the Sistine Chapel, and with the figures signifying Pity and Terror looking over her shoulders. Reynolds's signature and the date may be faintly noted on a strip of embroidery at the edge of the tunic; it was only the second painting he ever signed. (The other signed portrait depicts Lady Cockburn and is now in the National Gallery in London.) The experimentation with bitumen to achieve a velvety undercoating to the canvas failed miserably; since the material has never completely hardened, cracks and lumps have formed in the darker part of the dress and background. The hands and face of the actress are, happily, unaffected.

Gainsborough's *Cottage Door* (c. 1780) was the third important purchase from the Westminster collection acquired through Duveen. Two months later, May 24, 1922, Duveen wrote: "I am pleased to inform you that we have purchased Turner's painting, *The Marriage of the Adriatic*—[now called *The Grand Canal, Venice*] (c. 1837)—which we discussed when we had the pleasure of seeing you. . . . I regard our acquisition of it as a great victory as it was until then the finest Turner in private hands in England."

Another letter soon followed, "I am much obliged to you for your favor of June first with regard to the Turner picture, but I notice that although you say 'the beautiful picture,' your letter is not very Turneresque and somewhat lacks the warmth of the picture itself! There is only one question which I would like to ask you, does Mrs. Huntington like the picture? Because if Madame does, then I shall not dispose of it until you have both seen it." The shimmering light on the water plus the swarms of people, including Shylock from Shakespeare's *Merchant of Venice*, made a busy, exciting scene that the Huntingtons found compelling.

In the midst of these huge transactions is a rather plaintive note from Huntington, "Dear Sir Joseph: I am very disappointed in the brochure for Romney's *Lady Hamilton* as it contains very little information compared with others that have been made for me. . . . You mentioned offhand a price of $125,000. How much less are you asking an old customer?" Lady Hamilton's beauty and appeal inspired Romney to paint her many times and there are two of these flirtatious portraits in the Gallery, one in a white turban and the other peeking out from under the brim of a large hat, both of them among Henry

Huntington's favorites. (Complementing these pictures, in the manuscript collections of the Library, is an amorous and cautionary handwritten letter from Admiral Lord Nelson to Lady Hamilton, most likely a 75th birthday gift to Huntington from his book dealer, Rosenbach.) Other portraits which Henry Huntington particularly liked were *Sarah Siddons*—admired because the actress had overcome such humble beginnings—and Raeburn's *Master Blair* (c. 1814), because the subject reminded him of his son Howard as a boy, just as Arabella was reminded of Archer's youth. *Master Blair* was the one painting seldom out of their company as it customarily traveled with them cross-country aboard the private car.

A year later, Mr. Huntington wired, "Of course shall be glad to see you and Lady Duveen. But doubt very much my ability to purchase any more pictures. Is the Reynolds *Duchess of Devonshire* [1775-76] among those you intend bringing?"

Duveen brought the painting on his next trip west. Huntington was eager to buy but, despite repeated efforts, a suitable location in the house could not be found. Close to midnight the last evening of the visit, when Duveen was resigned to taking the lady back with him, George Hapgood, Mr. Huntington's secretary, had a brilliant idea. They roused Duveen's two assistants from slumber and together covered an alcove in the main hallway. Poised there, the Duchess greeted Huntington as he came down the stairs to breakfast. Duveen's bill for $525,000 was presented May 15, 1925. The portrait is now shown in the far end of the main exhibition hall.

Fame of the collection spread and many, including the actors Douglas Fairbanks and Ethel Barrymore, asked to come see it. Duveen, justifiably proud, was eager to comply, but during Mrs. Huntington's lifetime, casual visitors were never welcomed. An exception was made in 1922, when Duveen asked if an old Huntington enemy, newspaper man William Randolph Hearst, could be invited to see the paintings. And, in May 1926, Duveen wrote, "This morning I paid a visit to Mr. and Mrs. John D. Rockefeller, Jr., and they told me that they were taking a trip to San Francisco in their car and will halt in Pasadena for two hours. If you are able to show them the collection personally, it will do me a great amount of good. . . . I will frankly tell you that this is a great opportunity for me to get nearer these people and a word from you will mean more than I can well express. . . . Privately, Mr. Rockefeller needs a little broadening out because he is always rather skeptical, and it would be doing a good thing for the world of art generally, and me perhaps particularly . . . because the sight of your collection would be an absolute revelation to him. So you will be doing him a good turn, and me a good turn at the same time. Pray do not laugh."

The day was a huge success as Henry Huntington reported: "I had a pleasant visit with the Rockefellers—there were eight in the party which included Mrs. Rockefeller and the three youngest sons. After seeing the house and the library, they staid [*sic*] to lunch, and altogether we had a most enjoyable time, and I was glad to have the opportunity to know Mr. Rockefeller better. I did you no harm in my conversation and told both of them that they should deal through you."

When Duveen visited San Marino he had many invitations from Hollywood people whom he had not met. One came from the actress Pola Negri, who asked him to the Ambassador Hotel for dinner. Alphonso Gomez related in his 1959 interview, "that was a kick for Mr. Huntington; he laughed to beat the band . . . the moment he heard that Duveen had received an invitation from the movies." The next day at breakfast Huntington was already prepared for his joking. But Duveen said, " 'You should never have sent me there. . . . Some of the stars approached me and they asked me if on the next trip when I come to see you I can bring some paintings, nice paintings $150 to $200, to hang over their fireplaces. . . . Now Mr. Huntington, you made me waste one solid evening.' "

In the library building are large portraits of Henry and Arabella Huntington. In the winter of 1923 telegrams had gone to San Marino from Duveen praising the artist: "Wonderful

artist here Sir Oswald Birley who has painted some great portraits in England. . . . You may be interested to know that he
has obtained recently a commission from Mr. J. P. Morgan [Jr.]
to paint his portrait." Huntington's portrait shows an astute,
dignified, rather expressionless gentleman seated in a Chip-
pendale-style chair, to signify his interest in English art and literature, and posed against the vaguely defined bookcases of
the paneled house library. Arabella's is an unforgettable
glimpse of a strong-minded woman staring directly from the
frame without pretense and with no vestige of her breathtak-
ing youthful beauty. She is seated in one of the eighteenth-century tapestry-covered chairs, placed temporarily in the entry
between the dining room and the small drawing room, to
show her devotion to the French decorative arts. Birley completed the paintings, after many delays, in May of 1924 in San
Marino. Not long afterward, the Huntingtons and their en-
tourage left for New York, where Arabella died a few months
later.

Huntington's bereavement did not deter him from future
purchases; in fact, the pace accelerated as his own health deteriorated. In 1925, Duveen brought to California Constable's
rich and impressive landscape *View on the Stour near Dedham*
(1822) and Gainsborough's seated portrait of his composer-
musician friend Professor Abel, painted circa 1777. Karl Fred-
erich Abel, who had studied at Leipzig, probably under Bach,
had been appointed chamber musician to the queen in 1759.
Gainsborough himself was an amateur player and skillfully
depicts his teacher with a viola da gamba leaning across his
knee and a white dog resting under the table. The composi-
tion, expression, and colors of the painting clearly reflect a
labor of love. Its sale was one of the first instances of a famous
picture leaving one American private collection for another
(via Duveen of course, who had purchased it from the George
Gould collection).

Despite a note from Huntington demurring, "Your letter
was very interesting but I want you to know that I think it is

not worth the trouble to bring out the 'Pinkie' Lawrence," this enchanting little girl became Huntington's final major addition to his collection. Pinkie's formal name was Sarah Goodin Barrett Moulton; her family owned prosperous sugar plantations in Jamaica but kept their ties with England. In 1792 the little girl and her two younger brothers, Samuel and Edward, were sent back to England to be educated, a long and dangerous journey involving many years abroad. Missing her dearly, her concerned grandmother wrote to a niece near London to commission a portrait of the child, then about eleven years old, "in an easy careless attitude." Thomas Lawrence, in 1794 a young artist at the start of his outstanding career, was chosen. He posed "Pinkie," the nickname probably referring to the diminutive size of his subject, against a low horizon, with the illusion of a gentle breeze blowing through her dress and the ribbons of her bonnet. Despite the grandmother's desire to receive the finished portrait, Lawrence recognized his success and asked that it might be included in the Royal Academy Exhibition of May 1795. A week before, "Pinkie," possibly the victim of measles, died, and there is no indication that the portrait ever made its way to Jamaica. Instead it was kept in England in the possession of family members, including Pinkie's brother, Edward Barrett of Wimpole Street (father of Elizabeth Barrett Browning), and was not publicly seen again until 1907, when it was again hung at the Royal Academy in an exhibition of Old Masters. Later it was sold to Lord Michel-ham and, when his collection was dispersed in 1926, Duveen was the buyer, paying the highest auction price on record, 74,000 guineas, or $377,000.

Pinkie, often considered a pendant to *The Blue Boy,* although they have no connection other than the depiction of remarkably handsome young people, invoked an unexpected letter from Duveen:

"I am endeavoring to write you a letter which I find the greatest difficulty in composing. It is one that you will perhaps be surprised to receive, and may regard it as a rather 'infra dig' on my part, but I am emboldened to continue because I gladly realize that our relations are not those merely of dealer and client. . . . Frankly then, this letter concerns 'Pinkie' which it now appears Mr. [Secretary of the Treasury, Andrew W.] Mellon wanted rather badly, and was under the impression I would offer to him. During my visits to Washington since I last had the pleasure of seeing you, he referred to it again and again, remarking upon the great likeness of 'Pinkie' to his daughter, and how sad he was to feel he could not get it, because of all the pictures he owns he coveted this the most. . . . If by any chance at all you think you could bring yourself to consider making what would be a really magnificent gesture in favor of Mr. Mellon, I would appreciate a line from you. After that, it would have to be done through you, for nobody but you could make the offer."

Huntington's answer to his old friend's request is dated April 13, 1927:

"My dear Duveen—It is rather difficult for me to reply to your recent letter about Pinkie. Besides doing something for you, I should like very much to be of service to Mr. Mellon,—in fact, in view of my admiration for him, there are few persons for whom I would like to do a favor more readily than Mr. Mellon. But the difficulty of the situation is that the picture really belongs to the Henry E. Huntington Library and Art Gallery, and not to me personally; for that reason, I shall have to put it before the Trustees. This I will do at the earliest opportunity. Although I really feel there is no question what their decision based on their own enthusiasm for the picture will be. I trust you will understand the situation and Mr. Mellon will also. With kindest regards to you, and to him when you may see him, I am, Yours sincerely, Henry E. Huntington"

Soon afterward, Henry Huntington left by private car for Philadelphia for an operation from which he did not recover. Since the loss of Mrs. Huntington, Duveen had shown his concern in letters and telegrams and frequent visits to San Marino. Duveen was involved in setting up the Arabella Huntington

Memorial Collection in a special wing in the library building. Henry Huntington had requested a collection of objects from the French decorative arts she loved so well, to include porcelains, tapestries, sculpture, and fine furniture. Duveen utilized parts of the George Gould collection, the Beauvais tapestries *Italian Village Scenes*, some of which he had previously sold the Huntingtons, and added pieces from his own large stock. One hall is arranged as a sculpture gallery. Jean-Antoine Houdon is represented with a fine marble bust of an elegant court lady (1777), formerly from the collection of Maurice de Rothschild, and the bust of the artist's own daughter at the age of four, *Sabine* (1791), from the George Gould collection, a sculpture which has come alive from a piece of flawed marble.

Arabella had willed her personal collection in New York to Archer, who had in turn presented much of it to institutions including the Metropolitan Museum of Art in New York, the California Palace of the Legion of Honor in San Francisco, and the Yale University Art Gallery. From Archer's inheritance Henry Huntington acquired a group of Renaissance paintings and furniture, which occupy the north wing of the memorial. There *The Madonna and Child* by the fifteenth-century Flemish artist Roger van der Weyden may be seen. Arabella had bought it from Duveen at the Rudolphe Kann sale in Paris; through negotiations with Archer, it came to San Marino. To pay for these final acquisitions, ranch land which had been devoted to orange groves was deeded to Duveen, land now divided to make an exceedingly attractive residential area.

Here the relationship of the two old friends comes to an end. Duveen lived on until 1939 although his activity lessened because of the Great Depression and his ill health. When he died at sixty-nine in his suite at Claridge's, he left the business to his two close aides, Edward Fowles, who had been with the firm since he had first answered a "Help Wanted" sign at age fifteen, and his own Oxford-educated nephew, Armand Lowengard. During World War II, Lowengard became a leader of the French Resistance and the Paris and London houses of

Duveen were closed. Fowles moved to America and carried on the New York business. But an era had ended and he could never maintain the old flamboyance. In 1964, Duveen Brothers was sold to Norton Simon for $15 million. Some of the items were dispersed, and the remainder forms a part of the Norton Simon Collection in Pasadena.

Duveen had accumulated many awards. He had been knighted in 1919, had been made a baronet in 1927, and in 1933 elevated to the peerage with the title Lord Duveen of Millbank, the London neighborhood which is the site of the Tate Gallery, which houses many of his benefactions. He gave millions to the Red Cross, National Gallery in London, and the British Museum, where John Russell Pope, who was the architect for the Huntington Mausoleum in San Marino, designed the wing Duveen donated to house the Elgin Marbles. His memory in this country is perpetuated by the pleasure of viewing the treasures that he loved at the Huntington Gallery and at other great museums across the nation.

The Library

"This library will tell the story. It represents the reward of all the work that I have ever done and the realization of much happiness."
Henry E. Huntington, *Los Angeles Examiner*, 1919

One of the first books Henry Huntington ever owned is kept in a special section of the rare book stacks of his Library, encased in a faded green morocco box. Entitled *Songs for the Little Ones at Home*, the volume is a selection of religious and other poems for children. The frontispiece is inscribed in his mother's handwriting with the date March 1859; Henry Edwards was just nine years old. In a letter to Henry Huntington, dated April 17, 1916, George D. Smith, the shrewd and aggressive dealer who early assisted him in buying many of the great libraries that make up the Huntington Collection, wrote to him in San Marino: "I am sending you the little book you asked me to have restored and put in a morocco case. They have made a fine job of it and I trust it will please you."

Although Henry Huntington had always been a lover of books, it was not until he was in his mid-fifties and came into his inheritance that he moved beyond the prescribed parameters of book collecting for gentlemen of his position—principally standard sets by standard authors in expensive leather bindings—into more focused and sophisticated spheres. In his early days as a young man working for his Uncle Collis in West Virginia, he had purchased books intuitively, impulsively, with no particular design in mind. When he bought out his sawmill partner there, $1,800 worth of books were part of the payment. In February 1883, when the Huntingtons were a struggling young family, Mary Alice wrote her mother-in-law: "Edward bought him a very handsome new bookcase." He went on to buy a considerable number of books when he was living in San Francisco in the 1890s.

But it was after his separation from his first wife, when he lived for several months at a time at the Metropolitan Club on Sixtieth Street and Fifth Avenue in New York, that Huntington began to indulge his enthusiasm on a grand scale. Visitors to his rooms at the club reported that every chair and table, as well as the floor beneath his bed, was covered not only with books and manuscripts but also a fine layer of dust because he did not want his prized possessions damaged by careless cleaning. In 1904 he purchased $15,000 worth of books from the dealer Isaac Mendoza and in May of the same year he wrote to his daughter Elizabeth: "I like to walk in the park but it is always so crowded on fine Sundays and I do so dislike crowds. I prefer to be alone with my books."

In 1908, the year he retired from many of his interests in the business world, Huntington purchased an 1896 reference work called *Rare Books and Their Prices,* noting in the margins the names of twenty-five landmark books and key authors from the Gutenberg Bible through Thomas Hardy. This would prove to be a skeleton guide for the rest of his collecting career, as he systematically sought out and bought the finest examples attainable of each item marked.

The 1908-9 Henry Poor sale, held at the Anderson Galleries on Madison Avenue, was the first auction in which Henry Huntington bought heavily, acquiring well over a quarter of the titles. He was (under the alias of Mr. Jones) represented at this five-month sale by the agent he had come to rely on almost exclusively—the blunt, scantly educated George D. Smith, a dealer who far preferred spending his spare time at the race track to reading the esoteric volumes he handled. A supersalesman, Smith had a phenomenal memory for title pages and prices paid by previous purchasers. Huntington, with Smith by his side, soon became a familiar figure at the auction house exhibitions, often prowling around the back room late at night, vigorously pointing out his selections to Smith. Balding now, with a thick, white, fastidiously trimmed moustache, and wearing a wing collar and large pearl stickpin, Huntington became known to the Anderson staff as "Uncle Henry."

In 1909 E. Dwight Church, a Brooklyn bibliophile, died, leaving a library that was, although comparatively small, rich in exactly the kind of material upon which Huntington was beginning to focus: English and American historical and literary works in first, early, and rare editions. Huntington, instead of taking his chances at auction or joining a syndicate, set a precedent for some of his most successful subsequent acquisitions by buying the Church collection en bloc in April 1911, for $750,000. He would go on to purchase, also en bloc, such important collections as those of Beverly Chew and Frederick R. Halsey, the Grenville Kane collection of Washington manuscripts, the Ward L. Lamon library of Lincolniana, and many volumes from the library belonging to the Duke of Devonshire; thus he acquired the achievements of whole lifetimes of collecting.

Among the choice English books he bought from the Church collection were eleven Shakespeare folios, fifty-five early Shakespeare quartos and first editions of Spenser and Milton, as well as the first edition of Henry Fielding's *Tom Jones,* consisting of six uncut volumes in their original boards and containing the Church bookplate. Huntington himself never used a personal library bookplate. Americana included the *Bay Psalm Book* of 1640, the first book printed in the American colonies; the *Eliot Indian Bible* of 1663, a phonetic translation into the Algonquin Indian language to be used in converting the native tribes to Christianity; George Washington's account of his genealogy, written in 1792 while he was President; and Benjamin Franklin's manuscript of his autobiography, begun in 1771 when Franklin was sixty-five and continuing to the year of his death at age eighty-four, containing various corrections and revisions by the author. Also acquired was a group of nine French and Flemish fifteenth- and sixteenth-century Books of Hours. Eventually he was able to collect sixty-eight of these delicately illuminated prayer books for his library.

The acquisitions from the Poor and Church collections were important, but an even more significant event in the building of the Huntington Library was the dispersal of the collection of Robert Hoe. Born into a family of printing-press inventors and factory owners—himself the developer of the color press—Hoe had been a passionate collector of books from his early youth and, at the time of his death, his Thirty-sixth Street brownstone in New York was cluttered with sixteen thousand early books, manuscripts, and incunabula; a listing of his pre-eighteenth-century books alone filled six closely printed volumes. The sale, which began on April 24, 1911 and continued for seventy-nine sessions, attracted to the United States for the first time all the most prominent antiquarian booksellers from abroad, such as Alfred Quaritch and Benjamin Maggs of London; Mme. Theophile Belin of Paris, whose expertise in illuminated manuscripts and incunabula was unsurpassed; Dr. Ludwig Baer of Frankfurt; the Americans Charles Sessler and the mysterious Belle da Costa Greene, bidding for J. P. Morgan; and Dr. A. S. W. Rosenbach, attending his first great buying event, with bids from the Wideners of Philadelphia burning holes in his pocket.

Also present at the opening evening session, making one of his rare appearances and wearing full evening dress, was Henry Huntington. In an obituary memoir for *The American Collector* in 1927, W. N. C. Carlton described the scene as follows:

"His bright searching blue eyes looked out in kindly and interested fashion on the scene around him, his sensitive, mobile mouth betrayed his thoughts when something amusing occurred or was said. Huddled beside him was George D. Smith, his chief agent and negotiator for book purchases— Smith, whose short, stout body and deeply stooped shoulders gave him an almost gnome-like look, and whose supreme self-confidence made him the boldest, most truculent bidder who ever sat in an auction room. An English visitor, looking at the two men, so strangely contrasted in character and physique, smilingly remarked, 'Don Quixote and Sancho Panza.' "

The unquestioned gem of the collection was the large, exquisitely illuminated, two-volume Gutenberg Bible, one of only twelve surviving copies printed on vellum and bound in fifteenth-century calfskin. It contained both the Old and New Testament and the Apocrypha, in the Latin text known as the Vulgate. The Hoe copy is illuminated with superb hand-applied historiated initials and brilliant marginal decorations. The first book printed with moveable metal type in Europe, this bible is the work of Johannes Gutenberg of Mainz, Germany, commonly regarded as the inventor of printing in the Western world.

As Carlton's first-hand observation continues: "The climactic moment came with Item 269, the vellum copy of the Gutenberg Bible, and a battle of giants ensued for the possession of this incomparable rarity. Smith opened with $10,000. When $20,000, the highest previous price brought by a copy was reached, a chorus of whispered ohs and ahs floated through the room. From that point on, George D. Smith and Joseph Widener wrestled mightily for the beautiful volume. When, amid a breathless silence, the great prize fell to Smith for $50,000, a burst of enthusiastic applause rang throughout. 'Who is the buyer?' A quick exchange of signals between George D. Smith and the auctioneer was followed by the announcement that the purchaser was Henry E. Huntington, whereupon the applause was renewed with great heartiness."

Huntington rose and took a bow. He had established a new record for the highest price ever paid for a book and the following day the *New York Times* proclaimed Huntington a figure of outstanding importance in the world of collectors.

News of the purchase produced accusations that Huntington had bought with wild disregard for real values and also produced an avalanche of letters from the general public offering him literary treasures, real or imagined. From his old friend, Epes Randolph, the engineer who had designed many of the routes for the Pacific Electric, came a tongue-in-cheek note: "Dear Mr. Huntington, I have known for many years that you were sadly in need of the influence imparted by a constant use of the Holy Writ, but I did not suppose that on short notice you would feel the need of $50,000 worth of it 'in a bunch.'" To which Huntington replied, in a similar vein: "My dear Randolph, . . . I found out after I had purchased it that I could buy one for 10c, the contents of which would probably have done me as much good as the one I have, so you can imagine how chagrined I felt that I had paid $50,000 for one." Huntington's purchase, considered outrageously extravagant at the time, has proved to be, on the contrary, an astute buy; in October 1987 Christie's sold the one-volume Doheny Gutenberg on paper to a Japanese bookseller for $4.9 million, with the auction house commission raising the price to $5.4 million.

Among the other great treasures obtained for Huntington from the Hoe Collection were *The Book of St. Albans*, for $12,000, and the Caxton edition of Gower's *Confessio Amantis*. The coveted Caxton edition of *Morte d'Arthur*, for which Huntington was the underbidder, went to J. P. Morgan. However, in the end, Smith had obtained for his prized client more than half the Hoe library in terms of money, or nearly one million dollars worth of books.

Smith's method of presenting the books was to send catalogues of forthcoming auctions to his clients with recommended lots checked and estimated prices penciled in. This material would be accompanied by a note filling in background information and detailing the reasons for his recommendations. Typical is this portion of a letter to Huntington dated March 6, 1913:

"I send herewith my letter postmarked copy of the Crane Collection. It contains some of the most important items of Americana offered in years. There are a few exceptional items we must have to go with the Church books. Number 69, Berkeley's Virginia, only two copies known, and this is the only one in America. It is very difficult to say what this book will bring as it is the most important and all the big libraries and collectors will want it. It is fully as rare as the Winthrop we got in the Hoe Sale. You should get it at almost any price in reason." Sir William Berkeley's *Discourse and View of Virginia* (London [?], 1663 [?]) is now one of the treasures of the Huntington Library.

In January, 1914, Smith engineered an agreement with Huntington to buy twenty-three volumes printed by William Caxton, the first English printer, and the Kemble-Devonshire collection of plays, including one of only two surviving copies of the first edition of *Hamlet* (1603), which, coincidentally, had once been owned by the famous eighteenth-century author and bibliophile John Phillip Kemble, brother of Sarah Siddons, whose portrait as *The Tragic Muse* by Sir Joshua Reynolds hangs in the Huntington Gallery. The price of the collection was $750,000, with $150,000 in cash and the balance in three notes of $200,000, coming due at four-month intervals.

After Huntington married his uncle's widow in 1913, most of his books were housed in the ornate mansion built by Collis and Arabella on the corner of Fifty-seventh Street and Fifth Avenue in New York. On the third floor of this fully fireproofed house, above the driveway, was the long and narrow library reading room, with a large table in the middle for displays, ceiling-high bronze bookcases, and two desks facing each other for Huntington and his secretary. One side of the room was dominated by a fireplace, to the right of which was a safe hidden behind a bookcase. Here some of the rarest treasures were kept. Towards the front of the house, with a window overlooking Fifth Avenue, was a smaller book room which held manuscripts. Huntington spent most of his time in

New York in the library room, looking over new purchases, planning future additions to his collections, reading his favorite authors, Dickens and Thackeray, and showing off his prizes to those who could appreciate them. Later, George Ellery Hale, one of the original Huntington Library trustees, would write in the *Los Angeles Times,* "His affection for his books and manuscripts was so intense that I have often seen tears come into his eyes as he talked or read aloud from some favorite passage."

Huntington's peak years as a collector coincided with a time in which there were exceptional opportunities in the rare book world. In England, in 1909, taxation laws were changed so that aristocratic families, whose libraries had been growing since the Renaissance, often chose to sell their books and papers to avoid increased death duties. Huntington also benefited from the disposal of important English libraries put up for auction in order to satisfy the heavy tax assessed after World War I.

Smith kept his eye out for the accouterments of book collecting as well, as enthusiastically reported in the *New York Times* magazine of March 19, 1916, which described "a remarkable bookcase . . . made of woods collected from forty different sources connected with Shakespeare's life or buildings or localities mentioned in his plays. Such a bookcase was delivered last week to the home of Henry E. Huntington, the famous collector, in New York City. It was purchased in Europe by George D. Smith, art dealer, and sold to Henry Huntington for $10,000." The price reported was an exaggeration of $4,000, very possibly based on inflated information provided by Smith. About two weeks later, Smith, playing on Huntington's competitive relationship with Henry Clay Folger, founder of the leading library of Shakespeareana in the United States, wrote to Huntington: "I enclose herewith a letter from Mr. Folger who is very anxious to get the Shakespeare bookcase I sold you. The case and set of books have been delivered to your 57th Street house. Do you care to sell the bookcase and, if so, at what price? I told Mr. Folger I doubted very much that you would part with it." Huntington ignored the letter, and the bookcase now stands in the Special Reading Room of the Library.

He was, around this time, becoming more and more intent upon the shaping and pruning of the collection. In 1915 he employed, at an annual salary of $6,000, George Watson Cole, who had previously worked at the New York Public Library and the Free Public Library of Jersey City. In the years between 1916 and 1924, a series of auctions of Huntington's duplicates and less valuable items was held at the Anderson Galleries, the proceeds of which—over half a million dollars— were plowed back into new literary material. Other books acquired in collective purchases (including such rarities as the two-volume first edition of Cervantes' *Don Quixote*, which he traded to Archer Huntington for his Hispanic Society in exchange for the much less valuable Thomas Shelton English translation) were also disposed of in an effort to concentrate the collection on British and American imprints.

A major coup was the 1917 en bloc purchase of the Bridgewater House library, an extraordinary family collection started in the reign of Elizabeth I, acquired by Smith through Sotheby, Wilkinson & Hodge. It had been founded by Sir Thomas Egerton, Lord Keeper of the Great Seal, who, under James I, was made Lord High Chancellor of England and elevated to the peerage as Baron Ellesmere in 1603. As a patron of the arts during the last years of the sixteenth century, Ellesmere had received many dedicatory first editions and important manuscripts and had bought numerous other books on publication. There is a rich archive of correspondence tracing the family fortunes, including letters signed by James I, Sir Francis Walsingham, Sir Francis Bacon, and Sir Robert Cecil; John Donne was the baron's secretary. The collection descended through generations of heirs, who also added valuable material, and brought it to Bridgewater House in 1803. On the death of the third Earl of Ellesmere in 1914, the entire collection of 4,400 printed books and about 14,500 manuscripts was sold for death duties.

The great treasure of the Bridgewater House library was a manuscript of Chaucer's *The Canterbury Tales*, on vellum, put together circa 1410, or about ten years after Chaucer's death. The most elaborately decorated manuscript of Chaucer in existence, it contains a highly important portrait of the author on a white horse, as well as portraits of twenty-two of the fictional pilgrims who relate their tales.

The Bridgewater House purchases came to Huntington through the submarine-infested waters of the Atlantic during World War I under the condition that all insurance risks must be met by the seller, with the additional caveat, "It is further understood and agreed that if a portion of said library is lost in transportation, the price to be paid is to be reduced proportionately for the remainder." The bill came to one million dollars, paid in four installments of cash and promissory notes.

Another major source of prime material was the Britwell Court library from Buckinghamshire, a vast assemblage of predominantly English and American works sold at Sotheby's between 1916 and 1927. The first portion, Americana from the collection of S. R. Christie-Miller, a descendant of the founder of the library, was sold en bloc to Henry Huntington before the sale. The session of the auction held on December 19, 1919, even more than the others, attracted the leaders of the book collecting world. George Smith, vying with Bernard Quaritch as agent for Henry Folger, reveled in obtaining the only known 1599 fourth edition of Shakespeare's poem *Venus and Adonis* for his prize client for £15,000, or $75,000. Referred to by the *New York Times* as a "literary speck"—it measured just 2" x 3" —*Venus and Adonis* was, during Shakespeare's lifetime, the most popular of his works. This unique copy had languished for centuries in a vermin-infested lumber room, covered with dust and broken bric-a-brac and hitherto unknown to book connoisseurs.

It became more and more evident that Huntington possessed in his book collecting as much competitive spirit as he had shown in other areas of his career. It was particularly apparent in the accumulation of the Shakespeare quartos. As early as 1916 the Library's holdings of early quartos, those published before 1623, outnumbered those of the British Museum and the Bodleian Library. Six years later, in 1922, when Henrietta Bartlett's extensive bibliography was published, Huntington was able to claim ownership in almost all of the original and early editions of Shakespeare's quartos and folios, proudly checking them off and adding thirteen that had been omitted but were in his possession.

To a lesser degree, he took the same kind of pride in other areas of his collection. In a letter of 1919 to George Watson Cole, Huntington referred to the fact that, with recent additions, the collection now included a total of 909 pre-Restoration English plays and masques as compared with the British Museum's 922. "It makes quite a reduction in the number of plays I have to secure," he wrote, "to be even with the British Museum." Smith acknowledged and exploited this competitiveness.

Despite his genius in joining great books to great collectors, George Smith had a serious character flaw—he liked to gamble at the horse races. In 1918 he received an affectionate letter from Henry Huntington on the subject, "I am very glad to see that you are going to sell your valuable string of horses, and I think that by doing so you will be able to keep in the book business. If you should have succeeded in the horse business, you would have been a wonder, for I think that there is hardly one in a hundred keeping at it who does not go 'dead broke' before they turn up their toes. I have lived in Kentucky too long not to have seen the fatal results." Smith replied, "Thanks for your kind interest in regards to the horses, I sold all of them at auction and although I think several sold below their value, I let them go. It was too much of a strain for me."

In March 1920, Smith died suddenly of a heart attack at the age of fifty, while working at the desk in his office at 8 East Forty-fifth Street, New York. He had been, along with Joseph

Duveen and William Hertrich, one of the key agent/advisers
in Henry Huntington's life, each of whom played a major role
in forming the collections in San Marino. Now it was Dr. A. S.
W. Rosenbach's turn, and he became the final member of this
influential quartet.

Rosenbach, known familiarly as the Doctor, possessed a
sensibility far closer to Huntington's than that of the unsophis-
ticated Smith. An elegant bachelor, Rosenbach had expensive
tastes and a broad-based background in book dealing. As a
child he had assisted his uncle, Moses Polock, a noted book-
shop owner in Philadelphia who also conducted an informal
salon of bibliophiles among a clutter of old volumes and
manuscripts. In contrast to Smith, who had left school at
twelve to work as an errand boy at the Dodd, Mead publish-
ing house, the Doctor had a Ph.D. in literature from the University of Pennsylvania and could converse confidently with
scholars and librarians. His skills assured entrée into privi-
leged circles where, through his friendship with the young
Harry, he met the immensely wealthy Widener family of Philadelphia. After both Harry and his father, George D. Widener,
met a tragic death on the *Titanic,* the widowed mother established the Harry Elkins Widener Library at Harvard. The
Widener commissions established Rosenbach's credibility and
honed his expertise at auction.

Occasionally during Smith's lifetime, Henry Huntington
had bought from other dealers. Rosenbach had made his first
sale to Huntington in May 1911, with an exquisite copy of William Blake's *Thel*. The two men shared an appreciation of the
visionary poet and artist which was unusual at the time; soon
after, Huntington purchased the great series of Blake watercol-
or illustrations for *Paradise Lost* from the Doctor. In October
1916 he bought, for $14,000, another fine group of watercolors,
illustrating Milton's *Hymn to the Nativity*. A month later, a variety of other pieces were added, including the Sunderland-
Jersey-Amherst copy of the famed 1466 Cicero *De Officiis* on
vellum, an early run of Connecticut laws, and the James Madi-

son-Alexander J. Dallas correspondence. In December of that year, there was yet another Blake acquisition from Rosenbach, the eight watercolors for Milton's *Comus*.

Rosenbach's success in buying for Huntington and the other millionaires he dealt with came from their mutual desire to preserve the great Anglo-American landmarks of history. His selling methods were highly personal and discreet. An emotional man when extolling his wares, Rosenbach was known to break down in tears when praising a favorite volume. Sales would be sealed with a handshake. As in Duveen's operation, clients' secretaries and other retainers were generously rewarded for news of their employers with such special gifts as fresh salmon and brook trout, birthday cigars from London, railway and theater tickets, and even access to a New York speakeasy. George Hapgood, Huntington's secretary, was remembered with a thousand-dollar check after he was called upon to intercept a shipment of fifteenth-century books in which had mistakenly been packed Rosenbach's original cost sheet. The Doctor never denied that he extracted healthy profits from his customers, but just how generous these profits were he considered to be his own business and not that of Huntington's librarian, Leslie Bliss, who had assumed Cole's position and who meticulously checked all invoices.

In view of their close relationship, it is not surprising that Huntington would turn to Rosenbach for advice when he was contemplating the building of a structure to house his valuable collection on the San Marino Ranch. Southern California was, at that time, a cultural wasteland, but Huntington's faith in the future of the area convinced him that his collection should be independently and perpetually housed in the agreeable surroundings of San Marino, rather than ultimately deposited in some established eastern institution. His decision had far-reaching effects, touching both the financial and political communities. Horrified, William Dunn wrote from California on March 13, 1919, to Huntington in New York that the public was under the impression that a large library was under construction: "This is causing us untold trouble as we are making our fight for life right now on the theory that you have to go down into your pocket from 30 or 50 thousand dollars a month for a long time to keep the properties in operation and that with your enormous gov't charges for income and other taxes you cannot carry the burden any further. On this theory the Railroad Commission is now making a careful survey of our property with a view to authorizing economies of various kinds or raising fares. Our men understand the situation and are keeping quiet and at present doing good work. All this extravagant library talk makes the situation almost unbearable and for that reason, I telegraphed you today asking your authority to contradict the impression that has been given out." But Huntington, now nearing the age of seventy, could wait no longer and the necessary capital was released from his extensive assets so that the planning of the building could began.

It was Myron Hunt, designer of the main house and other Huntington properties, who was entrusted with drawing the plans after a visit to libraries in other parts of the country. Every detail of the construction was thoroughly discussed and on October 30, 1917, Huntington wrote to his architect, "I do not like the facade of the plans for the Huntington Library. It looks altogether too 'squatty,' lacking the dignity I want it to have. This plan has been up in my library in front of me for some while and I have tried my best to like it but I can't. The more I look at it, the less it appeals to me." Hunt continued to revise his plans and, in February 1918, Huntington wrote again, "The south and west end of the plan I think are all right. . . . Of course I should like some way of getting out from the Director's Room without being seen but there is plenty of time to decide."

Remembering the destruction caused by the San Francisco earthquake and fire to his uncle's art collection, Huntington insisted that special precautions be taken, such as constructing the bookcases that would sway in a temblor without buckling, and laying the floors in grids topped by heavy, unsecured squares of glass. (As early as 1906, Huntington was quoted as remarking to William Hertrich, "I am going to give something to the public before I die, but I shall house it so that neither earthquake nor fire can destroy it.") A spur of the Pacific Electric was built on to the grounds to carry in building materials, as had been done for the gardens and the residence.

Ground was broken in 1919, and the building completed late the following year. An outstanding feature was the two massive pairs of bronze doors cast with replicas of twenty-two famous printers' marks in bas relief. Following Huntington's preference, the signs begin with Caxton, the first printer in the English language, followed by Rastell, Wyer, Whitchurch, and others. The doors were made by the John Polachek Bronze and Iron Company of Long Island City, New York, and Henry Huntington was provided with an elaborately monogrammed silver key.

Leading the emigration from New York to San Marino in September 1920 was a group of Huntington employees and their families, which included eight couples, three bachelors, and nine children. Even though the building was not finished, the move was planned for early fall to coincide with the beginning of the school year. The first cases of library materials to travel west contained the books considered most replaceable: reference works, twentieth-century editions, and the Far Western collections. The more valuable books and manuscripts would remain in New York until the completion of the rare book room. In San Marino, the work of unpacking and checking off titles began immediately, before the books were arranged on shelves in the basement of the Library.

George Watson Cole, the Huntington librarian, arrived later, delayed by an appendectomy. He was responsible for hiring the other members of the staff which, dictated by the wishes of Huntington, was exclusively male. Huntington wrote to Cole that for reasons of his own he objected to females working in the Library, even though wages for male employees would be higher. It was not until after Arabella's death and just before the Founder's own that the Library admitted a woman to its ranks. Age, on the other hand, was never a barrier—Cole was sixty-five when he first joined the Library staff.

At the same time, in London and New York, the pace of acquisition continued unabated, effected almost exclusively through Rosenbach but with a few later major collections coming in from other sources.

In February 1921, Rosenbach set out for California to consult with Huntington about his bids for the 1922 Britwell sales. While there, he sold the collector, among other items, one of the most important pre-Shakespearean tragedies, Thomas Kyd's translation of *Pompey the Great* (1595). Then, poring over the catalogue with the Doctor, Huntington marked so many items that the two decided to make a private en bloc offer before the sale, but this time Sotheby's declined. Nevertheless, 175 items, or over half the sale, went to Huntington. The Battle Abbey Rolls, ninety volumes recording deeds, registers, and charters of Norman England, was one of the prizes bought by Rosenbach for Huntington, who paid $32,000 plus sixty first mortgage bonds of the Safety Insulated Wire and Cable Company. The Doctor added twenty other early English manuscripts in the deal.

The same year, the Wakefield Cycle of the Towneley Plays was purchased. This collection comprised a group of thirty-two short medieval miracle and mystery plays, including "The Second Shepherd's Play," that had been performed in Yorkshire during the last years of the fifteenth century by groups of traveling guild players. The only manuscript in existence of these plays, the Wakefield Cycle provides an important source for the study of medieval drama.

Also in 1922, the collection of Robert Alonzo Brock was bought directly from the heirs for $39,000. These letters, books, and pamphlets represented a lifetime of acquisition by this Virginia gentleman-historian, who had a rare opportunity to acquire them at the close of the Civil War when many of the old Richmond families needed money and a safe place to keep the material that had been in their hands for generations. Robert Schad, a member of the Huntington Library's original staff, deemed the purchase "one of the best bargains ever," as the 204 cases sent to San Marino contained some early Washington letters, Thomas Jefferson's 150-page manuscript notebook written when he was a young law student, orderly books of the Revolutionary and French and Indian Wars, and many deeds and papers, including four letters of Collis Huntington's. Another manuscript of family interest, purchased from the Anderson Galleries in 1921, was a proclamation of Thanksgiving commemorating the rescue of the country from "imminent dangers" following the treason of Benedict Arnold. It was signed by Samuel Huntington, President of the Continental Congress, in October 1780.

By 1923, the Library interior was almost completed and the collection was beginning to be used by readers. When Arabella Huntington departed for her annual late spring return to New York that year, her husband accompanied her reluctantly, writing to Dr. Coley, his kidney specialist, "Needless to say I should like to remain here for many reasons: the Library is in a most interesting stage, the large room being finished and new books unpacked." To Duveen he wrote, "We expect to leave in early June. Mrs. Huntington anticipating it and I regretting it."

Although the focus of the Library was now set and the majority of the great collection in place, the pace of acquisition did not decelerate. The fact that Huntington's health was beginning to fail seemed, on the contrary, to have lent an urgency to his buying. He purchased at this time several extensive bodies of manuscripts that would prove to be of particular interest to scholars. Of the sixteen thousand papers of the Campbell family, descended from John Campbell, fourth Earl of Loudon, who served as commander-in-chief of the British forces in America from 1756 to 1758, some ten thousand form an invaluable source for the study of Colonial America and early American military history. They were purchased from Sotheby's with the help of Duveen in 1923 and 1924.

The Stowe Collection, detailing eight hundred years of British history through the archives of the Temple and Grenville families in Buckinghamshire, was bought through the Museum Book Store in London in 1925. The storerooms of the grand country house belonging to these families yielded fascinating papers on subjects ranging from the mundane (cooking, gardening, a governess's school report concerning the younger children of the first marquis) to more complex matters of commerce and science; there was even an important political index grouping members of the Irish Parliament according to their degree of support for the government. The Stowe Collection of 350,000 items comprises the most extensive British family archive in the United States, and presents a unique portrait of the life of an aristocratic English family over many generations.

Other late purchases from Rosenbach were the famous King-Hamy-Ellsworth portolan map of 1502, one of the first world maps to show America and attributed to Amerigo Vespucci; a superb, richly illuminated manuscript atlas by Agnese; the manuscript bible of Bishop Gundulf, which was entered in the catalogue of Rochester Cathedral as early as circa 1130 and written in the second half of the eleventh century; and the Wilberforce Eames Collection of American imprints, consisting of thirteen thousand pieces gathered together to illustrate the beginnings of printing in the various states and territories of early America. Following this transaction, Rosenbach informed the press that the formation of the Huntington Collection in such a short span of years was "a greater achievement than the building of the pyramids or the Panama Canal."

In May of 1925, Rosenbach wired Huntington that he was coming west once more to discuss "some marvelous Shakespeareana from greatest private collection in Europe." Huntington agreed to put up $350,000 for fifty books from the collection formed in the mid-nineteenth century by Robert Stayner Holford—books which were still in London and not yet paid for by Rosenbach. Among the treasures obtained from the Holford Collection were the second edition (1594) of *Venus and Adonis*, the Foligno *Dante* of 1472, the Venice *Dante* of 1477, and the Milan *Dante* of 1478.

The following autumn, Huntington entered Lankenau Hospital in Philadelphia for surgery. Rosenbach was in constant attendance, doing all he could to facilitate the recovery of his client. After the operation Huntington celebrated by buying a miscellany of incunabula for just under $100,000, spending almost twice that amount the following spring for another group. These purchases, added to those acquired from other dealers, brought the number of books from the earliest period of printing (1455-1501) to approximately 5,400, making the incunabula collection at that time the largest in America. From 1920 to 1927 Rosenbach had assisted Huntington in sales amounting to $4,333,610.

The final major purchase Huntington was to make was the Hastings-Huntingdon Collection, which came via the English dealer Ernest Maggs, just two months before Huntington's death in 1927. It consisted of some thirty-five deeds, many dating back before 1600, court rolls beginning in 1644, and the all-encompassing correspondence of wealthy and distinguished members of the Hastings family. Thanks to the British practice of permitting public documents to remain in the private hands of officials, these papers were available for purchase.

When Huntington died in May that year, his obituaries called him the foremost book collector of his time, and counted his library the largest ever put together by a single American. The purpose of his mission seemed to reach far beyond personal aggrandizement. As he told a *Los Angeles Examiner* interviewer in 1919, "These books of mine in value to the world of thought are a great responsibility. The owner of such things is really little more than a trustee and his responsibility is far greater than attaches to ownership of an article there is some reason for regarding as purely personal."

The Gardens   VII

"I tell you, Hertrich, I have seen no place as nice as the Ranch."

Henry Huntington, Paris, October 5, 1913,
to William Hertrich

The Huntington Botanical Gardens cover 207 acres. Most of the area is open to the public but about 70 acres are not formally developed. These back areas give a glimpse of what the Ranch was like during the early days of this century, rather different from the carefully pruned and planted setting for the treasures of the Huntington Library and the two art galleries which we see today. When bought by Henry Huntington, the place was little more than a sparsely covered hillside topped by a vandalized frame house and surrounded by some mixed orchards and isolated live oaks. It took a special vision, patience, and expertise to convert the Ranch land into today's glorious complex of botanical gardens that delight and instruct half a million visitors annually.

William Hertrich and Henry Huntington first entered into a business relationship late in 1904 when, by great good chance, Hertrich was given a letter of recommendation to George S. Patton, Sr., General Manager of the Huntington Land & Improvement Company, then also in charge of the San Marino Ranch, earlier called the Los Robles Ranch. Huntington had bought the property the previous year from the Farmers and Merchants Bank, which had foreclosed on the mortgage of J. deBarth Shorb.

The first man hired to lay out and landscape the grounds had proved dishonest and the job was again open. Early in 1905, Patton wrote to Huntington, "The name of the new gardener at Los Robles is William Hertrich. He seems to be competent and is doing well." The opportunity was a dream come true to Hertrich, then aged twenty-six.

He had been born in Baden, Germany, where his father operated a ferry boat. After attending the local schools, he studied horticulture and agriculture on an estate in Dornbirn, Austria. Hertrich's early days are not well documented and he was a proud and sensitive man who shunned personal publicity. But it is obvious that most of the skills required for laying out the Huntington Gardens, supervising the property, and propagating thousands of plants were self-taught. He was an orderly man, a prodigious reader, an avid learner, and his attention to detail is evident in every field he entered. He was a perfectionist and his association with another decisive and energetic man, Henry Huntington, had far-reaching results.

In Hertrich's book, *The Founding of the Huntington Botanical Gardens*, he tells us that he spent his first three months in becoming familiar with every section of the Ranch property in order to visualize possible landscape improvements. Thus when Huntington returned to California, questions regarding the development of the property could be answered with some degree of certainty. Hertrich's conscientious study was typical of the way he worked and made a favorable impression on his practical employer.

The first years were extremely busy ones, spent modernizing the facilities and adding color and content to the surroundings. Huntington did not want the natural beauty of the land destroyed with formal plantings. He loved the majestic live oaks and built around them wherever possible. Pruning was forbidden in order to preserve the original shapes and growth patterns, surgery recommended to restore diseased trunks and branches, and small oaks were even allowed to spring up amid the orange groves. Fully grown shrubs and flowering trees were brought in that would bloom during the winter and early spring months when the family would be in residence. Work began on the road system, the irrigation network, and the fences, some of which were covered with climbing pink and white Cherokee roses with extra long thorns to discourage trespassing. A twenty-six-room dormitory went up for single male employees, south of the present San Marino City Hall.

Huntington and Hertrich were both careful spenders who saved the smallest items and checked and rechecked all invoices for accuracy. As Hertrich writes in his book, "Many opportunities presented themselves whereby I could have made a percentage on a sale. I recall one transaction in particular which amounted to seven hundred dollars. The party in question offered me 15% commission on completion of the sale. I declined to accept it, but suggested that he deduct this amount 'from the Old Man's bill.' About two years later, while discussing costs of certain items with Mr. Huntington, some of which seemed excessively high, there was occasion for me to remark jokingly that thus far I'd not accepted any personal commissions on any items. With a sheepish smile, he commented, 'I know, Hertrich, instead you've had it deducted from the Old Man's bill.' "

Plans for the new residence, to be situated on the same scenic hilltop as the original home, were drawn up as early as 1904 and perfected over the next few years. The three-story Victorian-style Shorb house had been built in 1875 with high ceilings and fine woodwork. When it was demolished, the building materials, including the nails, were salvaged and used again to erect six small cottages for married employees. One of the fireplace mantels is now in the Library, in a conference room adjoining the president's office.

The lily ponds were the first developed area, landscaped with exotic plants. Giant water lilies (*Victoria reginae*) from the Amazon, their pads strong enough to support a child, flowered out-of-doors until mid-January for the first time in Southern California, when heated water was supplied to the ponds. Now smaller water lilies fill the lower ponds, blooming during the warm summer months. A clump of papyrus, native to the Nile and used by the early Egyptians to make their writing material, grows at the edge of one of the ponds. Another pond contains the East Indian lotus, considered sacred in the Buddhist religion, which flowers in August. Some of the fifty species of bamboo in the Huntington Gardens surround portions of the lily ponds. To the north of the ponds is a new feature, finished in 1978, a sparkling, recirculating waterfall that rushes down the hillside, its mist and humidity aiding in the growth of subtropical plants. Below the waterfall, an ancient ombu tree, a native of Argentina planted by Hertrich in 1912, stretches high above its swollen roots like a giant pachyderm.

In 1905, to beautify the main drive coming up to the house above the lower orange groves, palms were collected throughout Southern California and from nurseries as far away as England, Belgium, Germany, and Japan. They were second only to oaks as Henry Huntington's favorite trees. Growth habits were compared to determine which would best adapt to use for residential and commercial properties and along roadways and rights-of-way in Huntington's subdivisions. The more tropical and shade-loving palms were sheltered and displayed in a lath house made of redwood slats arched into a circular dome one hundred feet in diameter. Today there are over two hundred species from many parts of the world. Those from the warmer tropical climates were removed after a few sub-freezing winters.

The desert garden was started at the same time as the palm collection and situated on the east side of the main drive, where there was unsightly erosion of the worn-out clay soil, which made it unsuitable for conventional planting. When Hertrich first approached Huntington with this project, Huntington recalled his painful contact with cacti in Arizona while supervising the construction of the Southern Pacific Railroad and vetoed the project. However, when told that two thousand different types of cacti were strictly American plants, that Southern California would be the one place where most of them could be grown year round, and that they could supply material for educational and scientific study, Huntington's instincts for collecting the unusual were aroused. He agreed to a half-acre trial plot; soon expanded, the garden now contains approximately five thousand species. Three railroad cars of plants were brought in from Arizona, including one with giant saguaros which perished in the freeze of 1937. Later over two hundred tons of red scoria (porous lava rock) were added to form a background to accentuate the beds of mammillaria (pin cushion cacti) along the center path.

In 1925, conversion of the lower reservoir and bird sanctuary added additional land, and now the desert garden encompasses over twelve acres. Arabella Huntington was earlier bothered by the hordes of mosquitos and requested that the lake with its boat and swans be filled in, but the work was not accomplished until after her death, when the lower orchards along Huntington Drive were sold and subsequently subdivided, and thus the reservoir was no longer needed for irrigation.

This arid, ugly hillside has now become a scene of surrealistic beauty and horticultural interest. Besides being a wonder to visitors, particularly those from countries outside the United States, the desert garden has the very practical purpose of testing plants new to cultivation. Starting around Christmas with the candelabra-shaped stalks of the aloes topped with orange, red, and yellow flowers, followed by the euphorbias, succulents which store water in their stems or leaves, and the tiny red to yellow flowers of the mammillaria, the desert garden is in bloom throughout the spring months. A display of succulent groundcovers, the majority from Mexico and South Africa, borders the east side of the main road along the garden. They are colorful and require little moisture—of importance to Southern California gardeners seeking to conserve water. Shipments have followed from all over the world as the staff makes expeditions to augment the collection. A glasshouse showing unusual and tender desert plants has recently been constructed near the top of this garden.

Next to be developed was the North Vista, planned at the same time as the residence by Myron Hunt. Seventeenth-century limestone statues depicting figures from ancient mythology, from the gardens surrounding the palace of the bishop of Parma, were acquired from P. W. French and Company in January 1921, for $31,500, to line the sweeping lawn which leads the eye to the great spraying dolphins of the Istrian stone fountain, against the backdrop of the San Gabriel Mountains. Here a profusion of camellias and azaleas borders the long allée—their color a joy in the winter months. Henry and Arabella Huntington played croquet on this grassy expanse.

The general layout of the extensive rose garden, on the site of the Shorbs' old peach orchard just west of the house, was also designed by Hunt. The architect, son of a distinguished Massachusetts nursery man, knew and loved trees and flowering plants and was skilled in their placement in landscape design. The first roses were planted in 1908 and covered twice the area they do today. The focus of the beds has become historical so that one may stroll through the paths and study the evolution of the roses in all their fragrant glory from the pre-Christian era up to modern times. There are thousands of rose plants to be admired, both bush and climbing varieties, in every variation of hue, all labeled to show when they were first grown, and how they were assembled—from commercial collections, private gardens, and even old cemeteries.

Never content with ordinary local material, Henry Huntington was ever eager to search out and test rarities of which he was both proud and possessive. Even rocks were special. Hertrich made the mistake of giving some specimens to Howard and received a cautionary letter from his employer: "We had the only kind of rock in that part of the country and to scatter it around makes it common."

In February 1909, Hertrich notified Huntington that he had mailed east "a list of very rare and choice cycads for which I have been inquiring all winter. These plants which are suitable for the courtyard would make the finest and rarest collection of any private plase [*sic*]. It certainly would be of more fame than any Italian garden." Cycads, distant relatives of the conifers that flourished in the time of the dinosaurs, are sometimes called "living fossils." They add only an inch or two of new wood each year so that a plant that is ten feet in height may be over one hundred years old. Soon fifteen were sent out from New Jersey and were much admired.

In 1913, Hertrich again wrote Huntington: "Yesterday I had the pleasure of seeing Mr. Bradbury's place in Monrovia. He is running a close race with us in the cycad line. . . . We got the best of him in a few varieties, and I will keep a close watch and see that he nor anyone else gets ahead of us in that line of plants. . . . If possible, please see the cycads at the Kew Garden, London, England; they are the finest in the world." When the Bradbury cycads came on the market, Hertrich won Huntington's agreement to the purchase price of $8,000. He then went to Monrovia to close the deal, taking along two wagons and six men—all concealed in the bushes a block from the house so that he would not appear too eager to buy, but close enough so that any agreement could be acted upon immediately, before Bradbury had a chance to change his mind. Half the hundred varieties in the world may be found today in the Huntington Gardens, clustered around the loggia of the main house and in the Japanese garden.

In the early days of the twentieth century it was fashionable for wealthy Americans and Europeans to add exotic pleasure gardens to their estates. Arabella had probably visited or read accounts of such plantings and was captivated by the novelty. An elaborate Italian garden on the south slope below the house was probably suggested by her, but it would have entailed a series of one hundred marble steps that would have been difficult to climb and treacherous when wet. Although plans for the Italian garden were never finished, a formal cutting garden was established for her use; it is now the site of the herb garden, west of the lunch room, and contains plants grouped primarily according to their usage—medicinal, cosmetic, culinary, and for various fragrances.

Henry Huntington was ever eager to please the woman he loved. In 1910, he decided to surprise her with a Japanese garden built on the site of a dammed water-retaining gorge, at the time overgrown with poison oak and wild grapevines and near the western boundary of the ranch on a tract of land recently acquired from George Patton. Huntington requested that the plantings look as though they had been there for fifteen to twenty years. Many mature trees and shrubs used in the landscaping were taken from the grounds of a commercial tea garden in downtown Pasadena owned by G. T. Marsh Co., Oriental art importers in San Francisco. The tea garden, then in financial straits, was bought in its entirety, including the old stone and metal ornaments. The house, its interiors imported from Yokohama, was laboriously moved in sections to its position overlooking the garden, its aged coloration blending in harmony with the beauty and spirit of the garden. Outlining the walks and ponds are huge boulders moved from the bed of the San Gabriel River with the aid of equipment from the Pacific Electric Company. A weeping willow bends over the ponds and a group of colorful koi flit through the water. The main entrance to the Japanese garden, guarded by two stone fu-dogs, is an unforgettable sight in late March or early April when the arbors of lavender wistaria are in bloom. The garden creates an illusion of much greater space than it actually occupies through the use of winding paths, constant shaping of trees and shrubs to maintain proper scale, and the serenity of water mirroring the surroundings. When the two white-flowered sweet olive trees are in blossom, an enticing perfume fills the air near the Japanese house, adding yet another dimension to the enjoyment of the garden.

In December 1911, Hertrich reported, "Have done a lot of work in the canyon since you left California. Have worked there nine hours myself everyday. . . . It was hard work for everybody to handle those big plants on account of transporting them by hand, down one side of the canyon, across the pond and up on the other side." Who can say what inspiration guided European-born Hertrich in the ancient and symbolic arrangement of the garden? He was helped in the physical work, however, by one of the Marsh employees, Toichiro Kawai, an experienced craftsman who reassembled the wooden components and later built the vermilion moon bridge, the smaller bridges, and the bell tower, traditionally put together with wooden pegs instead of nails, to house an eighteenth-century gong from a Buddhist temple.

Hertrich knew that the uniqueness of the garden would delight Huntington. He wrote in January 1912 that the Japanese garden is "beginning to show some character. I can assure you that there is nothing like [*sic*] in this country when I get it all complete." By March 1912, the first photographs arrived in New York and elicited the following reply from Robert Varnum, Huntington's secretary at that time: "I think you have created a joy forever. It seems like a beautiful dream, and I congratulate you on a great achievement. Mr. Huntington is tremendously pleased, but characteristically says, 'Oh well, I knew he could do it.' "

Behind the Japanese house, a three-room smaller wooden house was built for the use of Goto, the Japanese gardener, his wife, Tsune, and their five children. On pleasant afternoons, Tsune would strike a small bronze gong; then, attired in an elaborate silk kimono, would ceremoniously perform the traditional tea ceremony in the garden for the Huntingtons' enjoyment.

The large Japanese house was not used or opened until 1958, when it was refinished and restored for public viewing by the San Marino League. The raked gravel meditation Zen garden, reached across a zigzagged bridge over a ravine to the south of the house and bordered by a row of ginkgo trees, was finished in 1968, as was the adjoining bonsai court of dwarfed trees and suiseki rocks, natural stones that suggest miniature landscapes.

The correspondence between Huntington and his super-intendent which started on January 5, 1908, shows the owner's enthusiasm for developing the grounds of his great estate. He always enjoyed the challenge of planning large projects—rail-roads, trolley systems, subdivisions, or his own extensive gardens and orchards. Huntington wrote in his own hand: "I was thinking that possibly you might build a fence inside the fence in the canyon where it comes near the wall and plant ever-green grapes on the inside fence which will prevent the stock from eating the grapes This is merely a suggestion and per-haps you can hide the fence in some other way is there room to plant scrubbery [*sic*] there are you taking up all the syca-more trees above the cactus garden Has the hedge been plant-ed around the ground back of the home I am not asking sug-gesting that it be done if it has not been done as you know best when to plant it. . . . Do you think you can finally get rid of the gophers I enclose a catalogue of cacti did you send it to me?"

Later, on October 8, 1908, he wrote Hertrich: "I would like to have you write me once a week giving a report of work being done during the week and of anything else which you think may be of interest to me." His search for excellence never diminished as the estate grew in scope and beauty: in July 1924 he wrote, "I am always glad to have news of the Ranch, all the changes and improvements on the Ranch and else-where interest me very much."

The Hertrich-Huntington letters, covering almost twenty years, are in the manuscripts department of the Library. The first ones are handwritten and, later, as the staff grew and the work became more complex, they were typed by a secretary. The only gaps occur during the months when Huntington was in Southern California, staying first at the Jonathan Club and driving out in an open surrey behind a handsome pair of chest-nut horses and, after 1914, at the newly finished house on the grounds. Mutual trust and admiration are ever evident.

No part of the grounds or buildings escaped Hertrich's attention as Ranch superintendent. On March 15, 1918, he wrote, carefully controlling his anger, to Mrs. Huntington: "In preference to having your nurse pick flowers, I would much prefer to have you call me up in the morning and I will have my men pick them and have them ready. . . . This morning your nurse and another lady were gathering flowers quite freely and I noticed that they picked quite a few camellias and some of the varieties we have only one plant." Another letter to Arabella, of January 24, 1919, was more conciliatory: "Dear Madam: I am very sorry to report the loss of the three tucans [*sic*], the two in the aviary which have been here for about five years and the one received from New York, which was kept in the back of the servants' cottage. . . . It may have been due to their inhaling smudgy air which was very prevalent for about a week during the cold period."

To the Hon. Henry Wallace, Secretary of Agriculture, Washington, D.C., went the following request on August 20, 1921: "Enclosed herewith list of cacti which we would like very much to have for planting at the H. E. Huntington Estate, San Gabriel, California (near Pasadena). . . . We have recently visited the cactus collection at Washington and were very much pleased with it. . . . In the collection were a number of duplicates which doubtless can be easily spared and we have taken the liberty of writing you about this matter." On September 6, 1916, a query went to Professor Hall, University of California, Berkeley, California: "Dear Sir: Under separate cover I am sending you a bunch of grass which is found growing very freely in Fresno County, along Big Creek in the mountains. I would very much appreciate it if you or any of the professors at Berkeley could identify it for me."

In 1917 Hertrich sent neighbor George Patton a recipe for ant poison—a mixture of sugar, arsenic, and honey. The same year it was his responsibility to write a letter of condolence to the father of a young ranch hand who was killed on a public road when his motorcycle was struck by a car. There were several serious accidents on the Ranch but never a fatality, a tribute to Hertrich's conservative management and good sense.

The Shakespeare garden, originally devised in 1957, was a small formal Elizabethan knot garden intended to complement the important Shakespeare collection in the Library. The area has recently been re-landscaped into a more spacious and romantic English country garden, centered by a rough stone bridge crossing a marshy dell planted with a profusion of grasses and water iris, and a colorful display of other flowers mentioned in Shakespeare's works. A graceful willow is newly planted, while some long-existing native oaks form a background. Winding paths lead from two domed wooden pergolas to the columned arcade of the new Virginia Steele Scott Gallery of American Art, which fills a once overgrown corner of land adjacent to the greenhouses and garage.

In the early days, Hertrich lived alone in the dilapidated old Shorb mansion. On the occasion of the twenty-fifth anniversary of the city of San Marino in 1938, he told of the view from the south veranda of the house, whence it was possible to see one thousand acres of citrus spreading out, an ocean of leaves, with the fragrant blossoms as white caps on the waves of green. Before long, his mother came to keep house, and they moved to a cottage in the midst of an isolated orange grove. He was then exclusively landscape gardener of the Ranch, earning seventy-five dollars per month, and was supplied with housing, utilities, and the milk, poultry, or vegetable products that were produced on the Ranch. After two years, he took over supervision of all Ranch work and also the other Huntington properties in the San Marino area, the Wentworth Hotel, now the Ritz-Carlton Huntington Hotel, and the Old Mill, built under the supervision of the Franciscan Fathers of the San Gabriel Mission, which served as a clubhouse for a nine-hole golf course adjacent to the hotel.

At one time Hertrich was responsible for twelve hundred acres. At first he managed half a dozen men; the number eventually grew to seventy, an international brigade who worked ten-hour days without the help of machinery. There were few holidays, no sick leave, and a hat was passed around to help cover funeral expenses for the workmen and their families. Tools were checked out at the beginning of the day and, if they were not returned promptly, the cost would be taken from a man's pay. In 1919 wages were raised a penny from twenty-nine to thirty cents an hour: union organizers were strictly prohibited on Ranch property. Hertrich banned all conversation with the "Boss" unless Huntington talked to someone first. There were orders that when Mrs. Huntington came out, everyone working nearby must disappear. Arabella herself was doubtless unaware of this restriction, for she was fond of and generous to all her house servants.

In the fall of 1906, Hertrich married Margarete Stritzinger, a German woman who had been working in Southern California as a housemaid, at a ceremony at the San Gabriel Mission, and they remained a devoted couple throughout their long marriage. The two set up house in the same small cottage surrounded by orange groves, but, in 1910, Huntington built them a comfortable home on Huntington Drive near Palmas Station, a Pacific Electric stop on Huntington Drive.

Construction continued after the main residence was completed; a stable, dairy barn, and milk house were built, plus the garage and equipment sheds and the building now used for the cafeteria (originally the bowling alley and billiard room). The first greenhouse was built in 1909 to house tropical plants, principally orchids, which were Arabella Huntington's favorite flowers. At one time there was a plan for a series of conservatories for her private use, to cost $150,000. However, just before coming to San Marino in 1914, she suffered an attack of nephritis and the doctors felt it inadvisable for her to visit the greenhouses or any other damp places. Instead, large bouquets of flowers were daily arranged for her pleasure in the house and on the loggia. Two more greenhouses were completed for the culture of rare tropical palms and the winter growing of roses and carnations. Smaller glasshouses provided vegetables and melons for family use, and mushroom beds were established in the basement under the garage.

Fauna were also cultivated in quantity. Hertrich made a pigeon house and set it on the roof of a small office building out of the way of predators and then exchanged cactus plants for six pairs of pigeons to produce squabs for table use. An aviary thirty-five feet high was stocked with four to five hundred rare birds, segregated according to their feeding habits. The interior of the large cage was finished in a rustic manner with rocks and stumps and a stream of water trickling through.

In a turtle pond just north of the aviary, one hundred diamond back terrapin were raised for soup. Turtles are still to be found in the lily ponds and are often seen sunning themselves on the banks. The ponds also contain small mosquito fish to control the larvae that were earlier so annoying. German shepherds were raised by one of the gardeners to provide security at night, and a deer park with a salt lick was laid out on three acres now occupied by the Library building. The first tenants were a pair of Oregon black-tailed deer given by Frank Miller of the Riverside Mission Inn; they bred so rapidly that homes had to be found for the large herd when planning for the Library began in 1919.

From a visit to Mount Lowe in the San Gabriel Mountains, where he often went via his cable incline and narrow gauge trolley cars, Henry Huntington brought home two tame gray squirrels that had amused guests lunching at the Alpine Tavern at the peak of the excursion route. The Ranch diet of avocados, nuts, and fruits agreed with them so well that their numerous offspring took over the neighboring communities and soon became a nuisance. For generations squirrels on the property appeared gray but sported red tails: a pair of red squirrels had been stowaways in a shipment of rare birds for the aviary. Most of the wildlife is still plentiful, perhaps less than when many of the gardeners had their own pet raccoons, but there are many skunks, possums, coyotes, birds, and migratory water fowl. Gophers abound, with a full-time employee setting traps so that their numbers will not get out of hand. Until a few years ago, a couple of deer remained on the grounds, in hiding most of the time but with an appetite for tender rosebuds. On July 8, 1913, Hertrich wrote, "I have not as yet bought any bees, but have made several inquiries concerning Italian bred bees. They are more gentle and much easier to handle. Also do not bother people along the road." Soon there was another addition to the variety of creatures enjoying the land.

Early in this century, avocados were a rare delicacy in California. The first commercial avocado grove in the state was planted at the Ranch from seeds of Mexican fruit brought home by Huntington from his club in Los Angeles. When three hundred seeds were collected, they were started in small pots and the plants then moved out to the fields. They were planted twenty-five feet apart in all directions to accommodate the height and spread of the branches. By 1957 the trees became too tall and the grove too isolated for commercial picking. Many were diseased, and were destroyed to make room for a larger, landscaped parking lot, but the few huge remaining trees are ornamental year round and sharp-eyed visitors can find a few fine samples of the fruit on the ground if they wander out to the north of the Library building in the autumn. The citrus orchards were also profitable; at one time there were eighty-five acres of citrus trees and, one peak year, 64,000 boxes of Valencia oranges were packed for shipment across the country. Huntington was very proud that the Ranch operation was self-supporting. Around the time of his death, the Ranch property was reduced from approximately 600 acres to the 207 remaining today and much of the orchard land sold for private homes. Commercial harvesting ended in 1968 when the citrus companies and packing houses moved out of the local area.

Hertrich was continually trying new varieties and different fertilizing techniques, and surely one of the reasons he made plans to acquire a small ranch of his own was to have a chance to further his avocado and citrus experiments. When he discussed this project with his employer, Huntington was amazed and displeased and suggested alternate means of attaining a personal estate through savings and investments. In 1931 the Library Trustees commissioned Myron Hunt to design Hertrich a fine house at 1600 Orlando Road, now next door to the home of the president of the Huntington. Margarete Hertrich complained that it was too large for just the two of them, as the Hertrichs had no children. The house is used today by the present director of the Botanical Gardens.

Hertrich's discovery of two camellias on the grounds in 1905, one of which, a Pink Perfection, survives off the North Vista, led to a collection of over twenty species and almost fourteen hundred cultivars, and to a three-volume publication, *Camellias in the Huntington Gardens*. Camellia plants were bought from local and Japanese sources and others were brought in with the plant material purchased with the Japanese tea garden. Later, after World War II, the shady camellia walk was put in north of the Japanese house. Among those plants developed and introduced by Hertrich is the formal, white double *Camellia japonica* 'Margarete Hertrich', which may be admired along this pathway every February. There is also a vigorous *Camellia reticulata* 'William Hertrich', introduced in 1962, with a seven-inch bright red flower, planted in front of Hertrich's former house on the grounds.

Records were kept measuring rainfall and daily temperatures, and identifying labels were placed on all plants when the gardens were first opened to the public in 1928. The severe freeze of 1913 had destroyed many rare plants but also yielded invaluable information on the cold-tolerance of the survivors. Hertrich was much embarrassed the winter of Arabella Huntington's first visit, for the avocado orchard she had heard so much about had frozen completely. In 1922 came another devastating freeze. Hundreds of bushels of oranges were lost. Henry Huntington conceded that his plan for underwriting part of the endowment of the grounds with the proceeds of the citrus crop would be impractical, as the soot and grime from the use of smudge pots would permeate the collections in the Library and

Art Gallery. The winds of March 1938 are still remembered with awe for the extensive damage they caused. Several of the magnificent old oaks have had their branches wired for protection from future turbulence or a possible earthquake.

Although Hertrich was strictly an employee of Henry Huntington, unlike his advisers in the fields of art and books, the Ranch superintendent was an irreplaceable partner in the formulation of the botanical collection. As Hertrich's activities increased, so did his recognition among botanists and horticulturists. Starting in 1905, he was asked to judge at flower shows and to donate plants for worthy causes. Some of his awards include prizes from the Southern California Horticultural Institute and the Cymbidium Society, the Garden Club of America Medal of Honor, the Pacific Coast Nurserymen's Association Cup, the American Horticultural Society Citation, and a huge, heavy gold medal from the Massachusetts Horticultural Society for "Eminent Service."

In 1913 there were rumors that the ranches in the San Marino area, then under county government, might be annexed by one or more of the neighboring communities. As a precaution, a number of Mexican families were brought in to work on the Huntington property and thus bring the number of people locally to five hundred, the number of residents required to qualify for incorporation. Hertrich was one of the original San Marino City Council members and he kept his position for twenty-three years. The site for the City Hall on the corner of Huntington Drive and San Marino Avenue, now the main intersection of the city, was donated by Henry Huntington. Hertrich served six years on the San Marino School Board, was a fire commissioner, and did much to beautify the city by planting palms, ornamental flowering trees, deodars, and poppies and aloes along the right-of-way beside the tracks of the red Pacific Electric cars.

At the reading of Henry Huntington's will after his death in May 1927, Hertrich learned of his bequest, "To my friend, William Hertrich, $25,000." It was Hertrich's sad duty to make the funeral arrangements and to act as an honorary pallbearer. The site for the mausoleum, atop a gentle rise, had been chosen several years earlier by Arabella Huntington on one of her rare walks amid the outlying orchards. Work by the architect, John Russell Pope, was already in progress by 1927, but the building was not finished until 1929. As Huntington had directed, the area around the tomb was planted with his favorite lemon eucalyptus, tall slender Australian trees with a thin white bark.

There were many decisions to be made as the Ranch grounds were being prepared for public viewing, in accordance with Huntington's wishes. It was necessary to make the buildings conform to state regulations requiring all doors in a public building to open outward. The water supply above the first floor in the Huntington Gallery was discontinued to avoid leaks that might be a source of damage to the art treasures below. Burglar alarms were installed, and Hertrich worked out a unique and practical scheme whereby qualified men on the grounds staff also serve as guards during the afternoon public hours.

Five years after the public opening of the Huntington gallery, it became obvious that the paintings were too crowded and that those hung above the double staircase, two Lawrences, a Raeburn, and a Hoppner, caused a viewing hazard. Myron Hunt was called in to submit a plan for the main exhibition hall, now situated where the kitchen wing formerly stood. It was the first area to be air-conditioned. James F. McCabe, superintendent of the Chicago Art Museum, gave advice on rearranging and coordinating the exhibits. One suggestion which was not acted upon was to build a long corridor joining the house and the Library. During the Great Depression, Hertrich volunteered, in view of the fact that the income from securities held by the Library was reduced and expenses curtailed in every area, to have his salary reduced by $1,000 a year. He was then receiving $7,500 yearly plus his house, garden produce, and all necessary water.

Hertrich had early made it a rule that no cameras, except his own, be permitted on the Ranch property. There are some five hundred of his photographs on file at the Library and several wooden boxes of 3" x 4" slides. His photographic zeal has provided an invaluable record of the evolution of the Huntington grounds. Hertrich photographed Henry Huntington many times but there is no picture of the two men together. Hertrich would have thought such a pose improper and presumptuous on his part.

With the advent of World War II, Hertrich had additional duties and problems. With the threat of bombing along the entire West Coast, precautions had to be taken to protect the valuable collections. Skylights in both the art gallery and the library were covered over, shutters installed over all air vents in case of poison gas, and staff members trained in air-raid procedures. The paintings and art objects were removed and fitted into packing cases, and Hertrich took the rarest books and manuscripts to a vault at the First National Bank of Denver for safekeeping. It was not until after the war that the large vault was completed in the sub-basement of the new north wing of the Library. With the scarcity of able men because of the war and the lure of high factory wages, the institution was chronically shorthanded and it was Hertrich's personal efforts that insured that the horticultural collection survived. He was intensely patriotic, both he and his wife having become American citizens in 1908, and was very proud to have been able to help the United States Air Force by propagating thousands of shrubs to be used to hide anti-aircraft emplacements in California. In 1944 he proposed establishing a collection of medicinal plants, to substitute for many varieties of herbs unavailable after the attack on Pearl Harbor. His German background was never discussed and he never spoke or wrote in German.

During the war years, approximately eight acres of old citrus orchards below the house to the south were replanted with one thousand young eucalyptus trees donated by the

Department of Agriculture, then investigating whether they could provide fast-growing building material. The test proved that the trees were unsuitable and the dense plantings became a fire hazard. They were thinned to a few of the most attractive specimens and interspersed with other small plants native to Australia and New Zealand; their brilliant blooms and the silvery leaves of the eucalyptus enliven the walk between the Japanese garden and the massive ombu tree that dominates the area below the Jungle garden.

After Hertrich's retirement in 1948, he came to the office every day to continue his writings and memoirs and to keep watch over his beloved gardens. He would walk from his home and, later, when his sight deteriorated because a sliver of bamboo had penetrated one of his eyes, he would be driven over by his constantly protective wife, so that he could spend the days among the greenhouses and the individual gardens that he had created. At the end of his life, he was very frail but continued his daily routine. Death came suddenly when he suffered a stroke at age eighty-eight in 1966.

Flags at the San Marino City Hall were flown at half-mast for three days, as was the flag on the Huntington grounds. A commemorative ceremony was held in 1968, when a bronze plaque was unveiled near the lily ponds, the first garden to be developed. At the dedication Margarete Hertrich was visibly moved by the recognition given her "Wilhelm" and confessed that there were times when she wondered whether the gardens might have been his first love.

There have been many changes and additions, yet the Huntington Botanical Gardens remain true to their original purpose of providing education and enjoyment and are maintained largely according to Huntington's and Hertrich's basic plans.

Arrangements for the Future   VIII

So teach us to number our days
That we may apply our hearts to wisdom
> Verse from the Psalms carved on the winter
> panel of the Huntington Mausoleum

On August 30, 1919, shortly after construction commenced on the Library building, Henry and Arabella Huntington signed an indenture formally stating their intent regarding their holdings to be located in San Marino, "to promote and advance learning, the arts and sciences, and to promote the public welfare by founding, endowing, and having maintained a library, art gallery, museum, and park." A later gift comprised the residence with its works of art together with the stipulation to the Board of Trustees that either or both of the Huntingtons could live there until their deaths. A little over two hundred acres were to be permanently retained as a setting for the main buildings and gardens. The rest of the Ranch land was to be sold for residential use, the funds to be added to other securities to form a permanent endowment.

It was specified that the Huntington Library could never be merged with another institution and, if such an attempt were formulated, title to all property would pass to the Metropolitan Museum of Art in New York. It was also ruled that rare books, manuscripts, and all the valuable art works should never leave the premises for display elsewhere but that photographic copies would be readily available. There was never to be an admission charge.

The independent and self-perpetuating Board of Trustees of the institution was made up of the five men closest to the Huntingtons; its membership still consists of able men and women who are leaders in the financial and cultural affairs of Southern California. The original members, chosen for life, were George Patton, neighbor and manager of the Huntington Land & Improvement Company; William Dunn, attorney, who was elected chairman; Archer Huntington, Arabella's son; Howard Huntington, Henry Huntington's son; and George Ellery Hale, who made up for his shorter acquaintance with the founder by his great energy and enthusiasm. An astronomer from the nearby Mount Wilson Observatory, Hale was interested in public and cultural affairs and as much a booster of Southern California as Huntington himself. Some of Hale's more grandiose suggestions (which were not, needless to say, acted upon) included building the Library in marble as a $4,000,000 replica of the Parthenon and expanding the scope of the institution to include all fields of knowledge, including chemistry and his own speciality, astronomy. Hale's energy and prodding, coupled with Huntington's more practical ideas and those of the other trustees, were mulled over for at least a dozen years.

In 1926, the first indenture was "altered, amended, and modified so as to establish a basis to prosecute and encourage study and research in original sources of history, literature, art, science, and kindred subjects . . . and generally to conduct an institution of educational value." This statement encouraged the use of the Library as a center for independent research with the obligation of providing both accessibility to and protection of the holdings. By this time there had been changes in the board. Howard Huntington had died of cancer in 1922 at the age of forty-six, leaving his wife Leslie and six young children. Although he was shy and did not possess his father's business acumen, Howard had been universally liked and respected and was active in the affairs of the Los Angeles Railway. William Dunn, "Dear Billy" of the light heart and valued skills, who died in 1925, was the second trustee to be lost. He was never replaced as co-executor of Huntington's will, leaving the burden to Huntington's sister, Caroline Holladay, who later carried out the assignment with competence and vigor.

After Arabella's death in 1924, Henry Huntington rapidly closed his New York office, put his substantial Brooklyn real estate interests on the market, and moved permanently to California. On January 1, 1925, when all of Huntington's assets were transferred to Los Angeles from New York, the value of his holdings, mostly in stocks and bonds, came to a total sum of just under $40,000,000.

Many of the contents of Arabella's New York house were sold by Archer, principal heir to his mother's estate, at auction through the Anderson Galleries in 1926. There Huntington bought some of the pieces now in the Arabella Huntington Memorial Wing of the Library. At a session on April 15, 1925, he had sentimentally acquired a group of late nineteenth-century European pictures of the Barbizon and related schools and some miscellaneous portraits that are now hung in the staff areas and the Friends' Hall off the Pavilion entry. A month previously, at the March 1926 sale, Duveen had obtained for his client two Chippendale tables, a dressing mirror, a clock, and two satinwood cabinets that had been in the second-floor sitting room of the New York house.

This last group of furniture was never under the ownership of the trustees of the Huntington Art Gallery. It was, in all probability, intended for the small cottage Huntington planned to build for himself on the grounds, and from which he hoped to wander about incognito during public hours, eavesdropping on visitors' comments. The large house would be open as a museum and he still entertained the vain hope that Archer might someday use the guest bungalow that Hunt had constructed for his use. Although Huntington had once, in a letter to his sister Carrie, called Archer "arbitrary," he never wanted to give the impression that his wife's son was unwelcome and never voiced his displeasure except in incomprehension at his ignored invitations and the impersonal public sales of Arabella's belongings. Max Farrand, the first Director, hoped that Archer would step down as a trustee, as it was awkward making decisions without his attendance at California meetings, but he remained on the board until 1945.

When the indenture was signed on April 23, 1927, establishing the west wing of the Library "as set apart and perpetually dedicated to said Arabella Duval Huntington" with securities and other properties assigned to it exclusively, only four of the trustees were present in California; Archer's signature had to be witnessed by a New York notary. One thousand Newport News Shipbuilding and Drydock Company 1st Mortgage six percent gold bonds par value one thousand dollars made up the endowment for the memorial. The same deed of trust also provided for the maintenance of the mausoleum.

Although outwardly robust, Henry Huntington had not been well since 1915, with constantly recurring kidney and prostate problems. He slightly modified his usual activities and brought into the household Alphonso Gomez, valet and nurse. The patient did not complain of ill health except when he was in New York and severe colds left him wrapped up like a mummy throughout much of the winter. His appearance was usually debonair as Arabella had made sure he always had a large supply of new suits on hand and cutaway coats to be worn at dinner time. The electrical engineer on the Ranch grounds, John Gombotz, had a secondary job of breaking in all new shoes, wearing them for a two-week period to soften up the stiff leather.

His problems worsened in 1925 and an operation which had been feared by both himself and Arabella was finally performed at the Lankenau Hospital in Philadelphia. Here his sister Carrie wrote the following cheering letter: "My dear Edwards, It is good to get such encouraging reports about you but I shall be truly happy when I see you again seated in your own library, in front of your card table, dominos spread out, snorting at long waists and short hair. I am not sure but that I would be willing to bob my hair if it would keep up your circulation."

There is a story about the hospital stay told by the daughter of Huntington's personal physician, Dr. Ernest Bryant. Duveen and Rosenbach were both concerned, and rushed over for the medical reports, since each had an overwhelming interest in the recovery of their patron. Huntington sent for them to see him together and, as they entered the room, they found him lying supine on the bed in a short white shift with his arms outstretched. Motioning the dealers to chairs on either side, he asked each what he was reminded of. Both were nonplussed with Huntington's answer, "I remind myself of Jesus Christ between the two thieves." For once the loquacious supersalesmen were silent.

The results of the operation were less than successful and prolonged bed rest at home was prescribed, under the close supervision of a tyrant of a nurse with the improbable name of Miss Maybe. During these months of enforced inactivity, a great deal of thought was given to arranging matters for the future.

Of primary importance was the selection of a director of research for the Huntington Library, and eventually Dr. Max Farrand was personally chosen by Henry Huntington. Farrand had a background that made him well qualified for the appointment. He was a Princeton graduate, having studied history there under Woodrow Wilson, and later became an outstanding authority on the United States Constitution. He spent a summer at age thirty-two in Wisconsin studying under Frederick Jackson Turner, whose theories on the frontier had great influence on the growth of the Huntington Library's collection of Western Americana. Turner became Farrand's mentor as well as good friend and came to the Huntington as the first research fellow in 1927.

After seventeen years teaching history at Yale and before coming to the Huntington Library, Farrand had retired to take the position as Director of the Commonwealth Fund, a foundation set up by the Harkness family to promote an exchange of scholars between Great Britain and the United States. In his forties he married Beatrix Cadwalader Jones, a well-known landscape architect who designed the great gardens at Dumbarton Oaks in Washington, D.C., some of those of the nearby California Institute of Technology, and those of Yale University, besides many for friends here and abroad. Beatrix was the niece and an heir of novelist Edith Wharton and was acquainted with many literary and artistic people of the time. Her frequent and famous hospitality on Orlando Road did much to bring about good public relations for the Library. Their house was the one originally planned by Myron Hunt as a guesthouse for Archer. It was moved in 1928 to the northern boundary of the estate and enlarged and landscaped at her expense. William Hertrich's pride and possessiveness did not permit Beatrix Farrand's expertise being used on the Huntington estate; however, she did design the garden around her house. One of the most delightful letters among the Farrand correspondence is from Edith Wharton, congratulating Max on his new post, "Do let me know more details as they develop. Will Mr. Huntington house you or will you have to perch?"

During the summer of 1926 Farrand came to San Marino for two months and talked to Henry Huntington about the organization of a great library: its policies, its tools of reference and secondary works, its research associates and assistants and their salaries, and the need for continuing additions of new material to supplement the existing rare books and manuscripts. It was up to Farrand to supply the figures for supporting the Huntington complex to insure its future. He first envisioned an endowment of some $20,000,000, of which $17,000,000 would be for research alone, enough to fund an extensive series of scholarly studies on Anglo-American civilization. His plans had to be scaled down as the market value of the final endowment was estimated at about $10,500,000, which would still put the institution among the foremost in the world at that time. (The exact amount was uncertain as the securities were from privately owned companies.) Farrand's salary was $12,000 a year with another $3,000 for expenses and a rent-free house, a very generous amount when compared with a top academic salary, about $5,000 in the 1920s.

It was Max Farrand who was responsible for converting the private collection into the world-renowned research institution. He took office in 1927, a month after Mr. Huntington's death, as Director of Research and in December 1933 was also appointed as the Director of the Library and Art Gallery, a position in which he continued until 1941, when ill health forced his resignation. The Library and Art Gallery managed to continue without a Director during wartime, with William Hertrich as Superintendent.

Huntington spent his convalescence mostly confined to the house and, for the first time, received visitors other than family and old friends to show off his collections—an outlet he had previously been denied as Arabella was adamant that her home not be turned into a public thoroughfare. On one occasion when he was showing his paintings, she threatened not to come down to dinner, "Edward, let's call this the last time. . . . It annoys me terribly to feel we are living in a public institution. Why allow them to come see? They will be laughing at me. I'd rather stay in New York." Another activity that continued through his convalescence was rearranging the books in the library room of the house and planning new roads within the Ranch as property was sold or traded off to Duveen.

Besides his work in assembling the Arabella Huntington Memorial Wing of the Library, Duveen was consulted on plans for a final resting place for Huntington and his wife and recommended the architect John Russell Pope to furnish plans for a mausoleum. Pope's ideas were received enthusiastically, "The model arrived in perfect order. It is indeed a great work of art, and I have never seen anything in modern architecture that appeals to me more than this does. It is a great classic and just the type I dreamed of. There is one suggestion which I would like to make, and this refers to the carved bas-reliefs: I feel that these should be done by a great sculptor . . . in a very low relief. . . . Naturally I should prefer an American. . . . What do you think of considering Miss Hyatt, who is now Mrs. Archer Huntington? Have you seen her Joan d'Arc in the French Chapel of the Cathedral of St. John the Divine?" Anna Hyatt was approached but declined the commission, saying she was not familiar with the type of work planned and doubted her fitness for such an important undertaking. Her forte was in depicting heroic, larger-than-life animals, especially her favorite, horses. One such monument, honoring Collis Huntington, near the Newport News Shipyard, is of a young man subduing a stallion, symbolic of his taming of the west.

Pope then chose John Gregory, who had the necessary training and experience and a "very sympathetic hand," to work on the four curved panels and the sarcophagus. He started immediately but Henry Huntington died before the tomb was finally finished in 1929. As with other Huntington construction, the mausoleum, of white Colorado Yule marble, was designed to be earthquake-proof, with deeply reinforced concrete foundations. The inner chamber is faced with marble reliefs showing the seasons of the year with a short quotation under each. Significantly, the winter panel depicts a lonely old man bowed over a book and seated back-to-back with an angel extinguishing the flame of life. The mausoleum, placed on the highest elevation of the Ranch, about a third of a mile north of the entry pavilion, became the prototype for Pope's later architectural triumph, the Jefferson Memorial in Washington, D.C. Although Pope never visited San Marino, his name is carved on the steps of the tomb, a clear acknowledgment of his pride in the purity of design of this memorial temple.

The Ionic order of Pope's classical columns around the circumference of the mausoleum is similar to the style of other columns that are part of the Art Gallery and on the south side of the Library building, giving a sense of unity to the establishment. The capitals have been echoed again on the new building that houses the Virginia Steele Scott Gallery of American Art, opened in the summer of 1984 on the grounds to the northwest of the main Huntington Gallery. Designed by Paul Gray, the 19,000 square-foot gallery was constructed with part of an approximately $15,000,000 gift from the Virginia Steele Scott Foundation; Mrs. Scott was a Pasadena heiress whose greatest wish was to share her art with the public.

This small gallery is divided between viewing and working areas by a glass-domed courtyard that is reminiscent of the marble-domed tomb on the grounds to the north. Henry Huntington's favorite piece of garden sculpture, Janet Scudder's charming *Little Lady of the Sea*, stands in the atrium of this courtyard. He had bought it in Paris on his wedding trip, expressing his own joy and emergence into a new life. Also under the many-faceted glass roof is a bronze cast of Anna Hyatt Huntington's *Diana of the Chase,* an exuberant figure drawing her bow skyward, on loan from the Fogg Museum at Harvard, an appropriate and spirited reminder of family achievements. Two life-size Great Danes, male and female, also by Anna Hyatt, stand guard at the entrance to the Scott Gallery. The pair were Arabella's gift to Henry Huntington one Christmas.

In the eastern half of the building, in a room for curatorial activities, stands Henry Huntington's impressive desk, a massive rolltop with a warren of cubbyholes. It had been brought down from his office at the Southern Pacific Company in San Francisco and, during his lifetime, had been in constant use in his Library office, now the Trustees' Room. Facing Mr. Huntington's desk in the Scott building is Hertrich's oak rolltop, equally massive with perhaps even more little niches and drawers. The desks are at home with other pieces of American furniture chosen to enhance the American art collection. Another sentimental piece of old office equipment is the large decorated iron floor safe from the hardware store in Sacramento run by Collis Huntington in partnership with Mark Hopkins during the gold rush period; it is still of service in the business department of the Library building. Huntington's well-used surveying tools, found in a cluttered apartment in the garage on the Ranch, are now kept on the top floor of the Library where the family correspondence is stored. The handsome bookcase from St. Albans, in cherrywood with carved panels, followed Mr. Huntington throughout forty years and was finally given to Hertrich when a place could not be found for it in the San Marino house. At the time of Hertrich's death it stood in his Orlando Road home and is now in use in a second-floor office in the Library.

The Scott Gallery of American Art, which contains examples of American art from 1743 to 1936, is an enlargement of the original Huntington concentration on predominantly British art. Until the 1980s, the Huntington offered little representation in the arts of this country except for some fine early American photographs, some Gilbert Stuart portraits, a Copley, and the double elephant folio of Audubon's *Birds of America*. Today Mary Cassatt's tender *Breakfast in Bed* and the majestic *Chimborazo* by Frederic Edwin Church are among the best-loved paintings in the new gallery. The handsome early nineteenth-century American mahogany card table by Charles Honoré Lannuier with the gilt winged figure and carved feet was part of the Huntingtons' house furnishings in 1914, although probably used ornamentally and not for their favorite card games. Two late nineteenth-century bronze busts of Civil War leaders are shown from the Huntington Collection—*Abraham Lincoln* by Leonard Volk, and *Robert E. Lee* by Philip Martigny, heroes whose courage and virtue had fired the imagination of the young Henry Edwards back in upstate New York during the years of the conflict.

Just as the contents of the original art gallery have been increased by many valuable additions since Huntington's death, so a room in the Scott Gallery was left unfinished after its completion, and in 1990 was opened to highlight a collection of works by Greene and Greene and other California craftsmen from the early years of this century, a joint exhibition of the Huntington and the Gamble House. The Southern

California Research Center of the Archives of American Art, a branch of the Smithsonian, is also located in the Scott Gallery. The Library collection also continues to grow. Photographs of the Dead Sea Scrolls, deposited in 1982, are available for the first time to all interested scholars.

After Henry Huntington's operation in 1925, and even with the best of care, progress was slow. With his son Howard and William Dunn both gone, occasionally Huntington would be driven downtown to his office to confer with his staff; despite his lifeling involvement with transportation, he himself never drove a car. He would take along a small lunch of cheese sandwiches carefully packed in a square Lipton tea canister. Emma Quigley, the secretary he had inherited from Dunn, tried to persuade him to go to the California Club to eat. He preferred the quiet of the office however, for, as he told Miss Quigley, at the Club he would be surrounded by men whom he did not know well and who only wanted something from him. His mail was full of requests from charities and offers of various books and art objects for sale. His replies became a standard variation on the theme that he was no longer interested in buying and could make no contributions; he was concentrating solely on the undertakings to which he had already pledged his support.

Rosenbach was warned that further trips west on his part would not be worthwhile. Duveen, exuding vitality, was still pushing purchases and making final arrangements for the Memorial Wing. He was always generous with his tips: the housekeeper Nora Larson would receive one hundred dollars from the dealer at the end of each stay, and Gomez always received fifty, which he once spent on a new blue suit. In appreciation of services rendered by the secretary George Hapgood, his sister was given a building lot, part of the land that had been exchanged with Huntington for art objects. Duveen would brush aside the suggestion that the retainers were adequately paid and would defend the lavish handouts by saying they were part of his lifestyle and no one could take away his hobbies. In March 1926 he arrived with a few pictures. Huntington wrote Carrie of a little strategy of his own, "He has a wonderful collection of miniatures that also appeals to me more [than the pictures] but he does not know that yet." After a few months of debate, seventy-eight of these delicate watercolors were purchased, a few on vellum, the rest on ivory, and many framed in diamonds and pearls. Special cases were made and they are now shown in the north passageway between the dining room and the main exhibition hall of the Huntington Art Gallery.

In the spring of 1927, his general condition failing, Huntington wrote a letter to his New York representative, E. A. Adams, "I have decided to come on East with Dr. Bryant to find out why the wound does not heal satisfactorily, and will leave probably Friday next. I am feeling very well otherwise, and as long as it is best to go, this is the right time in view of the approaching hot season in the East. I shall go directly to Philadelphia." Gomez and Hertrich both remembered that Mr. Huntington felt particularly cheerful embarking on this trip aboard his private car, in contrast to the depression he had felt before the previous operation. His affairs were in order and he was ready for whatever the future might bring.

On May 5, 1927, a second operation was performed at the Lankenau Hospital. The cancer had spread and the seventy-seven year old patient had not the stamina nor the will to continue. Despite his weakening condition, he was able to glance briefly but proudly one day at a catalogue of English books printed between 1475 and 1640, of which he held the majority. Dr. Rosenbach stood by, offering words of encouragement and delicacies from his gourmet kitchen in nearby 2010 DeLancey Place. He kept the staff in San Marino informed of all progress and on May 17 advised Leslie Bliss, librarian: "He does not respond to treatment and his temperature is around 101, showing some disturbed condition." A telegram followed a few days later with the information that Henry Huntington had died on the morning of May 23, 1927. His last words, accompanied by a faint smile, had been a cry for Belle.

A special train was provided by the Union Pacific to return the body home. At Colton near San Bernardino, California, it was transferred to the Southern Pacific. At Shorb Station in Alhambra the private car, draped in mourning, was transferred to the Pacific Electric Railway and thus taken into the Ranch grounds. A troop of San Marino Boy Scouts, who had often benefited from Huntington's generosity, met the car and a youthful bugler sounded taps as the other boys stood stiffly in salute. The body lay in state in the house library for three days amid a profusion of flowers before the funeral took place on May 31. It was conducted by Dr. Robert Freeman of the Pasadena Presbyterian Church and limited to one hundred and fifty invited guests. There were many honorary pallbearers, made up of family members and business friends, and seven active pallbearers, who had been chosen for their length of service on the estate grounds. At 11:00 in the morning, the time of the funeral, all cars of the Los Angeles Railway and the Pacific Electric Company came to a halt, the employees of the Newport News Shipyards put down their tools, and the flags in Los Angeles and San Marino and on the Ranch were at half-mast. After the short, simple service, only close relatives and servants followed the bronze casket to the temporary gravesite near the unfinished mausoleum where it was placed alongside that of Arabella, and both were covered with a pall of orchids and lilies of the valley.

The will, drafted in 1925, had been read a few days earlier as it was necessary for business to proceed without delay. There were bequests to all the family, with his three daughters and sister Caroline Holladay each receiving a million dollars. The Huntington daughters in 1924 had received trusts of $150,000 each in addition to monies earlier given. At this time, Leslie, Howard's widow, was given a similar amount in exchange for the reconveyance of her house. Leslie was remarried to an investment counselor, James Rudolph Brehm, and she was given permission in the will to occupy the big home on nearby Hillcrest Drive for the next ten years. Five of Howard's children received $150,000 in trust with the youngest, Henry Edwards II, receiving a namesake's bequest of $200,000. Each of the three Huntington daughters plus Howard's children shared in the residue. Two million dollars went toward the development and enlargement of the Pasadena Hospital, now called the Collis P. and Howard E. Huntington Hospital, and there were many smaller bequests to relatives, servants, and institutions.

There is a saying that no man is a hero to his valet. The relationship with Huntington was an exception to the rule, for Gomez worshiped his employer and, at his own death in 1959, left instructions that a bouquet of roses be placed before the Mausoleum. His taped recollections have added remarkable insight to the personal life of the Huntingtons despite a certain naïveté and some lapses of memory. Another devoted staff member, Max Gschwind, grounds foreman under Hertrich, visited the tomb daily until his ninety-first year. Huntington was also remembered with affection and respect by those who worked under him: an assistant back in Kentucky wrote years later, "I am proud to be able to say I worked for him three years without being fired. But I did not work half as hard as Mr. Huntington. He never stopped working."

Henry Huntington was able to amass a multitude of unique treasures; his assembled collections in their incomparable setting are unlike any other in the world. When he found his Eden in Southern California, he decided that he had had enough of traveling and started making plans to leave his legacy to all the people even before taking up residence there.

This gentleman, with his basically simple tastes, his love of family and country, had lofty standards. His library of libraries was built up in a comparatively short time through a system of en bloc purchases that had also served him well in the transportation business. The British paintings came in more slowly, since they were acquired to fill existing parts of the house: Henry Huntington never purchased merely for the sake of value in the eyes of others. In the gardens as well, duplicates and inferior material and those outside his strictly established confines were sold or traded, leaving only the best examples. Duveen, Smith, Rosenbach, Hertrich, and certainly Arabella lent their suggestions, but the final decisions were always those of one man.

Accumulating, for Henry Huntington, was a prerequisite to sharing. He saw to it that the gardens were early opened to botanical groups under Hertrich's guidance, and accredited scholars were welcome to use the Library even before the books were fully unpacked and shelved. And today it is to be hoped that the Huntington dream will progress well into the next century and beyond, to instruct and inspire those of us who enter the paradise of a generous and farsighted man.

Bibliography

Beebe, Lucius. *Mansions on Rails: The Folklore of the Private Railway Car*. Berkeley, 1959.

Behrman, S. N. *Duveen*. New York, 1952.

Best, Gerald. *Iron Horse to Promontory*. San Marino, 1969.

Birmingham, Stephen. *California Rich*. New York, 1982.

François Boucher. Exhibition catalogue, 1986-87, Metropolitan Museum of Art. New York, 1986.

Brown, Dee. *Hear That Lonesome Whistle Blow*. New York, 1977.

Bruccoli, Matthew J. *The Fortunes of Mitchell Kennerly, Bookman*. New York, 1986.

Carlton, W. N. C. "Henry Edwards Huntington, 1850-1927: An Appreciation." *The American Collector*, 4 (August 1927): 165-70.

A Century of American Sculpture: Treasures from Brookgreen Gardens. New York, 1981.

Clark, Kenneth. *Another Part of the Wood: A Self Portrait*. New York, 1975.

Cole, Cornelius. *Memoirs*. New York, 1908.

Coleman, Charles M. *P. G. and E. of California: The Centennial Story of the Pacific Gas and Electric Company, Inc*. New York, 1952.

Crump, Stephen. *Ride the Big Red Cars*. 5th edition. Corona del Mar, Calif., 1970.

Duveen, James Henry. *The Rise of the House of Duveen*. New York, 1957.

Easlon, Steven. *The Los Angeles Railway through the Years*. Anaheim, Calif., 1973.

Evans, Cerinda. *Collis Potter Huntington*. Newport News, Va., 1954.

————. *Arabella Duval Huntington, 1851-1924*. Richmond, Va., 1959.

Fads and Fancies of Representative Americans at the Beginning of the Twentieth Century: Being a Potrayal of their Tastes, Diversions, and Achievements. New York, 1905.

Fowles, Edward. *Memories of Duveen Brothers*. London, 1976.

Friedricks, William B. "Henry Edwards Huntington and Real Estate Development." *Southern California Quarterly 71*, (Winter 1989): 327-40.

————. *Henry Huntington and the Creation of Southern California*. Columbus, Oh., 1992.

Galloway, John Debo. *The First Transcontinental Railroad*. New York, 1950.

Gimpel, René. *Diary of an Art Dealer*. New York, 1966.

Heller, Joseph. "Picture This." *Connoisseur*, October 1988.

Hoving, Thomas. "101 Top Collectors." *Connoisseur*, September 1983.

————. "The Berenson Scandals." *Connoisseur*, October 1986.

Myron Hunt, 1968-1952: The Search for a Regional Architecture. Exhibition catalogue, 3 October-8 December 1984, California Institute of Technology. Pasadena, 1984.

Huntington, Archer. *To My Mother.* New York, 1925.

Lavender, David. *The Great Persuader.* New York, 1963.

Lewis, Oscar. *The Big Four.* New York, 1938.

Littlefield, Susan. "Dumbarton Oaks." *House and Garden,* December 1986.

Maher, James T. *The Twilight of Splendor.* Boston, 1975.

Marcosson, Isaac Frederick. *Little Known Master of Millions.* Boston, 1914.

"The Multimillion Dollar Belle." *Artnews,* 84 (Summer 1985): 86.

Norris, Frank. *The Octopus.* New York, 1901.

Newton, A. Edward. *The Amenities of Book Collecting.* Boston, 1918.

Pope, Arthur Upham. *Archer Milton Huntington: Last of the Titans.* Privately printed, 1956 (?)

Rosenbach, A. S. W. *Books and Bidders.* Boston, 1927.

Rouse, Parke, Jr., "The Huntington Woman." *Westways,* December 1978.

Saarinen, Aline. *The Proud Possessors.* New York, 1958.

Sherwood, Midge. *Days of Vintage, Years of Vision,* 2 vols. San Marino, 1982-87.

Simpson, Colin. *Artful Partners: Bernard Berenson and Joseph Duveen.* New York, 1986.

———. "The Bilking of Jules Bache." *Connoisseur,* October 1986.

Sitwell, Nigel. "The Queen of Gems Comes Back." *Smithsonian,* January 1985.

Starr, Kevin. *Americans and the California Dream, 1850-1915.* New York, 1973.

———. *Inventing the Dream: California through the Progressive Era.* New York, 1985.

———. *Material Dreams: Southern California through the 1920s.* New York, 1990.

Thomas, Alan G. *Great Books and Book Collectors.* New York, 1975.

Towner, Wesley. *The Elegant Auctioneers.* New York, 1970.

Walther, Susan Danly. "The Virginia Steele Scott Gallery at the Henry E. Huntington Library and Art Gallery, San Marino, California." *Antiques,* August 1986.

Williams, John Hoyt. *A Great and Shining Road: The Epic Story of the Transcontinental Railroad.* New York, 1988.

Wolf, Edwin II, with Fleming, John. *Rosenbach: A Biography.* New York, 1960.

Index